Barnsdall Park

A New Master Plan

for Frank Lloyd Wright's

California Romanza

Written by Melanie Simo

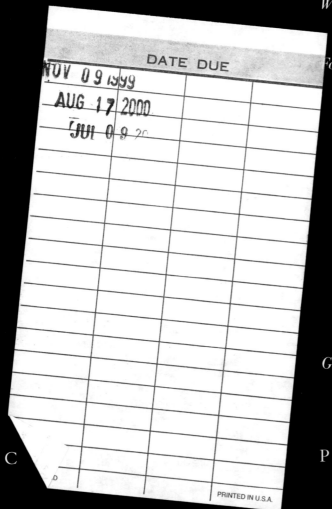

Foreword by Kathryn Smith

Graphic Design by Sarah Vance

S P A C E   P R E S S

Washington, DC

Cambridge, MA

Barnsdall Park Master Plan was prepared by
Peter Walker William Johnson and Partners

for the
City of Los Angeles
Department of Recreation and Parks

With input from the
Barnsdall Park Board of Overseers
Focus Committee on the Barnsdall Park Master Plan

Peter Walker William Johnson and Partners
Peter Walker, William Johnson, Tom Leader, Mia Lehrer,
Paul Sieron, Bruce Jett, Esther Margulies, Pamela Palmer,
Shelby LaMotte, Tim Harvey, Dirk Johnson

Consultants

Lehrer Architects
Michael Lehrer

Levin and Associates
Brenda Levin, Kathryn Smith

Kosmont Associates
Charles Loveman, Tim Sales

Many individuals assisted the master plan
team during the development of the new
plan for Barnsdall Park. Foremost among
these, members of the project focus
group volunteered their time and efforts
to help craft a new vision for the Park.
Membership included: Ari Sikora, Robert
Harris; Al Nodal, and Dr. Earl Sherburn
of the Department of Cultural Affairs,
Michael Devine, Cheryl Johnson, Cooke
Sunoo, Kit Neimeyer, Jeff Lambert,
Dwayne Wyatt, Heather Dalmont of
Councilwoman Goldberg's office,
Roxanna Tynan, Tom Reese, Ellen
Melinkoff, Susan Foley Johannsen, and
Jerry Cohen. In addition to serving on
the focus group, the following individuals
provided assistance in project manage-
ment and research to the study team:
Julie Riley, Department of Recreation
and Parks, Project Manager; Virginia
Kazor, Hollyhock House Curator and
Department of Cultural Affairs Archivist.

Special thanks must be extended to
the staffs of the programs of The Cultural
Affairs Department of the City of Los
Angeles, Barnsdall Park, particularly
Harriet Miller, Director of the Junior
Arts Center, Noel Korten, Director of the
Municipal Arts Gallery, Richard Ellis,
Director of the Barnsdall Arts Center,
and Thomas Albany at the Gallery
Theater for assistance in organizing feed-
back from program personnel as well as
in the orchestrating of workshops and
meetings.

Contents

Frank Lloyd Wright, preliminary sketches of street elevations for Olive Hill, 1920

Foreword

Kathryn Smith

As Frank Lloyd Wright's Hollyhock House (completed in 1921) celebrates its seventy-fifth anniversary, it is very fitting that the new *Master Plan for Barnsdall Park* takes so much of its inspiration from Wright's original plan. It also is appropriate to note that the park will celebrate its seventieth anniversary, a milestone that is marked by a rededication by the City of Los Angeles to the public spirit of Aline Barnsdall's gift. Especially gratifying in the realization of this master plan has been my participation through the office of Levin and Associates for Peter Walker William Johnson and Partners and Lehrer Architects. As consultant to the Historic Site Survey, I have worked in a cooperative relationship with landscape architects, architects, planners and economists to provide a holistic vision for Barnsdall Park. Most important, the support of the Departments of Recreation and Parks and Cultural Affairs has been crucial to the realization of the Historic Site Survey.

Of all the public places in Los Angeles such as the Getty Museum and the Huntington Library where art, architecture and landscape come together to form a sum greater than its parts, Barnsdall Park is the least known. While the historic buildings of Hollyhock House and the Barnsdall Art Center (formerly Residence A) have been published internationally and the Municipal Art Gallery and Junior Art Center continue to attract a loyal following, a wider audience has yet to discover Barnsdall Park. Although structures have been built and landscaping planted over the decades, there has never been a comprehensive master plan that integrates all the diverse facets of this cultural treasure: the interface between the public and private zones, the historic background and contemporary context, the conservation of its buildings and the restoration of its plant material. All of these elements are addressed in this volume.

During the joyous days surrounding the official dedication of the park in August 1927, Aline Barnsdall made a rare public statement explaining her donation to the City. "Who will care who Aline Barnsdall was fifty years from now?" she asked. In answering her own rhetorical question, she provided the objective that underlies the guiding spirit of this plan, ". . . what is important is a Park (representing city government) concentrated constructively on the creative, artistic side of life . . . ." She further clarified her intentions when she stated, " I gave this park not only as a gift but as the expression of an idea, and what I care most about is (that) this idea—labeled Barnsdall Park—shall live and develop with the years." More than half a century has passed since Aline Barnsdall made this statement and we are now able to determine how right she was. The reader of this volume will find that what is important is the *idea* that is Barnsdall Park. It has been rediscovered and made tangible by Peter Walker William Johnson and Partners.

Kathryn Smith
May 1996

Kathryn Smith is the author of
Frank Lloyd Wright, Hollyhock House,
and Olive Hill: Buildings and Projects
for Aline Barnsdall. *New York:*
Rizzoli International, 1992.

Lloyd Wright, elevations, perspectives, 1921. Top to bottom: Vermont Street, Hollywood Boulevard, Hollyhock House

Barnsdall Park

A New Master Plan

for Frank Lloyd Wright's

California Romanza

Melanie Simo

Introduction

On December 23, 1926, the heiress Aline Barnsdall deeded to the City of Los Angeles the summit and upper slopes of Olive Hill, in East Hollywood. Her gift, including about eight acres of gardens, groves, orchards, and a house by Frank Lloyd Wright, was offered as a park for the arts and, ideally, as a dreamlike setting for a child's artistic development. In the hopeful vision of its donor, the park was meant to grow in cultural significance, eventually to contain a theatre as well as an art club and recreational center, all clustered on a unique little hill from which the qualities of beauty, truth and freedom would radiate. Inscribed on the park's dedicatory plaque to the donor's father, T.N. Barnsdall, were the lines: "Our fathers mined for the gold of this country. We should mine for its beauty."[1]

For Aline Barnsdall, beauty was an essential quality of life. In her travels, she had come across some of the world's finest expressions of beauty: in theatre, in urban gardens, in architecture and in art. She had also recognized a kind of beauty beyond the world of artifacts, beyond the reach of human efforts to extract, bend, mold, shape, and give objective form. Beauty lay also in the natural landscape: in the splendid scenery of mountains, plains and oceans, and in smaller elements of nature—even a little hill. Her first sight of Olive Hill, a mound covered with olive trees, rising above a sweeping agricultural plain bounded by distant mountains, must have been striking. Here was a land form of great distinction, only slightly altered by human intervention, standing apart from, yet related to, a magnificent, larger environment.

The story of how that mound of olives became Barnsdall Park is a story of layering, of one conception of use and beauty laid upon another, over long periods of time. Reversing the process, one could try to peel back some of those layers (as the current master plan intends to do), and yet never peel back far enough to see Olive Hill as Barnsdall and Wright saw it in the beginning: a noble portion of earth, an object in itself, to be respected and, with sensitivity, to be shaped for a range of human needs. In the following pages, the narrative will run backward and forward in time, tracing these alterations, while the hill remains a constant, the focus of our attention and the real subject for restoration and renewal.

In 1927, a year after it was deeded to the City, Barnsdall Park was expanded to encompass nearly eleven acres and a second house by Wright. More of Barnsdall's original 36-acre property of Olive Hill became accessible to the public. And, as the nearby boulevards and avenues were developed with bungalows, duplexes, and institutional and commercial buildings on flat terrain, Barnsdall Park grew more distinct: still rural with its orchards of maturing olives, yet growing in dignity as the groves of young pines and eucalyptus flourished on the summit, framing views up to the buildings and outward from them. Over the years, the lower slopes of Olive Hill were developed with a hospital, apartment buildings and shops, while cultural enterprises were developed on higher ground. This was the evolution of a community for which Hollyhock House remained the focus and spiritual core.

With the Depression and the second world war, however, maintenance standards in Barnsdall Park declined. Aline Barnsdall died in December, 1946. As the post-war economy improved, her heirs and the City Fathers added new structures, commercial and cultural, on Olive Hill. Parking lots were added and, in the forty years since the Park was established, more than three quarters of the trees of Olive Hill were gone. Urbanization spreading from the multiple centers of the Los Angeles region reached the slopes of Olive Hill. The cultural life of Barnsdall Park was renewed with exhibitions, renovations, and a new Municipal Art Gallery, yet the environmental quality suffered, as reflected in the relentless loss of trees and expansive views. In time one could drive down the broad boulevards of East Hollywood without any awareness of the park; as a rural and cultural community, it had become further isolated, a retreat largely obscured by buildings.

With the irony typical of postmodern life, it was the Metropolitan Transit Authority's proposed new subway construction in the early 1990s, requiring a temporary staging area at the base of Olive Hill, that would provide funding to revitalize the Park. A new master plan for Barnsdall Park, prepared by Peter Walker William Johnson and Partners, of Berkeley and Los Angeles, with the assistance from the City and several associates, now offers a new vision, surely as hopeful as Barnsdall's original gift, yet different in its recognition of changing circumstances, social, economic, and environmental. In essence, the new plan proposes strategies for restoring and refining the landscape, along with measures for new interconnections, reaching out to a more diverse public than Barnsdall could have imagined.

Before attempting to honor the vision of Aline Barnsdall, the planners and designers tried to understand that enigmatic woman, whom Wright considered "as domestic as a shooting star." Wright worked with her on and off for nearly ten years, winning her admiration but not her full confidence or cooperation. An aspiring theatrical producer with avant-garde notions of drama, Barnsdall was uniquely prepared to commission and finance a series of experimental works by Wright. They first met toward the end of 1914, when, beleaguered by personal and professional crises, Wright needed a sympathetic, promising client. A change of scene—even faraway Southern California—was welcome. As with a free-form musical composition, or "romanza," he played with exotic architectural forms that might evoke the region's pre-Columbian traditions. His predilection for the interweaving of structures and landscapes led to compelling forms of haunting beauty. But within a decade, both client and architect would be frustrated, embittered. What went wrong?

The 1910s and 1920s have long been considered years of transition, or "lost years," for Frank Lloyd Wright.[2] His work for Aline Barnsdall and other clients in Los Angeles has found some champions, some detractors. Reyner Banham saw Wright's work in Southern California in the 1920s as intriguing products of his "wilderness years," when the self-exiled Midwestern architect found himself in collision with previously unknown cultures and traditions.[3] Barnsdall, less rooted in any one place, was not exactly an exile as she confronted the unknown. An American of European tastes, Yankee enterprise, and pioneer instincts, she sought freedom for her artistic and social experiments in a still developing region of great natural beauty. For her, as for Wright, Southern California would be an adventure. At a time when Hollywood was still a village, attracting people with extraordinary talents to engage in its local industry of dream making, both Wright and Barnsdall were drawn there to realize dreams of their own. Inevitably, in such an environment, one risked disappointment for the sake of something marvelous, untried, unknown.

To appreciate the challenges faced by both Wright and Barnsdall, each is viewed separately here, much on their own terms. But a sense of place—the land—must come first.

East Hollywood looking southeast, circa 1901

The Land

Before the phrase "Pacific Rim" entered our language, another term was used to denote the land masses lapped by waves of the Pacific Ocean—the "Ring of Fire." Linking New Zealand, Japan, Alaska, and the Pacific coasts of the American continents is a ring of volcanic mountains and faults: earthquake-prone areas where instability is a permanent state and disaster is both memory and threat.[1]

Frank Lloyd Wright first encountered this precarious ring in mid-career. From 1913 to 1922 he worked on the Imperial Hotel, in Tokyo, a commission that entailed several ocean voyages and long periods of time away from his Chicago office, while he struggled to design a structure that, among other things, could withstand the fury of a major earthquake. In this he succeeded. On September 1, 1923, when the Kwanto earthquake struck, his building stood while countless others succumbed and over 100,000 people lost their lives.[2] At the same time, working within another segment of the "Ring of Fire," California, Wright built a house and center for the arts on Olive Hill that have outlived the Imperial Hotel; yet they have suffered some earthquake damage over the years. Collisions of tectonic plates have occurred somewhere beneath the apparently solid ground, just as collisions of temperaments, expectations, and priorities had occurred between Barnsdall and Wright. As client and architect were continually traveling around the globe, communicating by letters and telegrams, the earth and ocean floors beneath them were no less mobile; they simply moved in different time scales, geologic time and human time.

We can now see that the imperceptible movements of the earth's elements, inching their own mysterious ways onward, are not simply metaphors for human activity. As John McPhee's friend Eldridge Moores reminds us, "Man is a geologic agent." The time scales may be incompatible, but the outcomes of earthquakes and, say, hydraulic mining are comparable in the millions of cubic yards of earth moved. Moores, a California geologist, specializes in plate tectonics—now the generally accepted theory of earthquake activity, first developed from 1959 through the 1960s. When Moores looks at a landscape, he sees layers of other, older landscapes beneath them; he carries a mental "portfolio of ancient scenes, worlds overprinting previous worlds."[3] This kind of vision could well serve designers and historians of the humanized landscape, as it once served Frank Lloyd Wright: not merely as a metaphor, but as yet another layer of understanding, added to our cultural, social, and economic ways of looking at the land.

Before moving on in human and geologic time, we might pause to consider the land as viewed by the namesake of Barnsdall Park, T.H. Barnsdall, a pioneer in oil drilling and mining. In 1860, twelve years after a gleam of yellow at Johann Sutter's sawmill turned out to be gold, the California Geological Survey was established. As scientists and engineers set out on expeditions, the state legislators, mine owners and speculators may have hoped for news of mineral deposits at least as impressive as the silver of Nevada's Comstock Lode, discovered in 1859. But curiosity led some scientists to observations of a different order. The state was vast by East Coast standards. The scale of natural features—trees, mountain ranges, peaks—was impressive, as was the apparent isolation of this land. To reach California, by sea or by land, was arduous and exhausting. And the region's isolation in social and cultural terms was matched by the isolation of its many microclimates. The Coast ranges, the High Sierra, ocean and waterways, deserts, varying rainfall, topography, orientation, some winds deflected, and some winds sweeping over broad basins, all conspired to increase diversity and also to isolate great numbers of plants and animals from one microclimate to another. The existence of what we now call "ecosystems" intrigued some scientists to search for patterns, theories, some connecting threads.[4]

California, a youthful land by standards of geologic time, offered evidence to support Charles Darwin's theories of evolution long before they were generally accepted in the United States. When *On the Origin of Species* appeared in 1859, Louis Agassiz, at Harvard, rejected Darwin's theory. Agassiz's student Joseph Le Conte found reason to agree with Darwin, however, after spending four years in California. Le Conte and his colleagues found geologic evidence that prehistoric marine creatures had once thrived in California; that the ocean had once reached the slopes of the Sierra Nevada range (thus covering nearly the entire state). Le Conte saw that evolutionary processes could have indeed been at work, processes that Darwin believed would require a degree of geographic isolation. This isolation also encouraged the growth of endemic species, such as Monterey Cypress and giant sequoia—species which, apart from human intervention, are only to be found in certain unique areas of the world.[5]

An ideal of isolation would be an island; and that is how, in 1510, the Spanish novelist Garcia Ordoñez de Montalvo imagined a place "very close to the side of the Terrestrial

Olive Hill crown looking north toward the Hollywood Hills, 1919.

Paradise." He called the island "California." A few decades later, when Hernando Cortes, Juan Rodriguez Cabrillo, and other Spanish explorers reached what is now Baja California and San Diego, they found neither gold nor anything approximating their ideal of paradise. They did find people we now call "Native Americans," some of whom practiced farming, while most did not; they lived on wild plants and nuts, small game and fish. Their ancestors are believed to have migrated from Asia, via the Bering Strait, some 30,000 years ago, during the Wisconsin Glacial Age.[6]

If all Americans are in effect immigrants, coming from somewhere else, the same can now be said of their land—or at least significant portions of it. Pursuing the theory of plate tectonics, scientists now speculate that southeastern Alaska may have drifted from Australia to Peru and then northward to its present location. Boston was once perhaps part of Africa. Northern Ireland may have once been part of North America. Perhaps at some time in the remote past, California did not yet exist. Rather, as tectonic plates shifted, pieces of terrane (three-dimensional pieces of the earth's crust), were gradually assembled and compacted, eventually colliding with the North

American plate. If so, then out of this collision, some islands we now call California gradually became mainland—perhaps about 29,000,000 years ago, when the Pacific plate first touched the North American plate where Los Angeles and Santa Barbara stand today.[7]

If the theory is valid, then most continents, or pieces thereof, were at one time interrelated. The story of the earth becomes one of movement, flux, collision, change. For their own psychological well-being, Moores suggests, human beings may want to believe that the prehistoric turmoil of flux and change is mostly over; that the stage is now set for human activity on mainly solid ground. Some have even declared California's San Andreas Fault a Registered Natural Landmark, as stated by a plaque outside the Almaden winery.[8] But that fault is still active, unstable. And what is a landmark if not a place that, by transcending the flux and change around it, gives us a degree of stability: a sense of where we are, who we are, what our roots are, or might be?

In the midst of Aline Barnsdall's peripatetic life and his own periods of escape and exile, Wright attempted to create a place of some stability: a home for her to return to and a center for the arts to flourish. In the relatively unknown, geologically and culturally youthful Los Angeles basin, there was Olive Hill—presumably once an oceanic island visible from the mainland of the Santa Monica or the San Gabriel Mountains—now a potential retreat, or sanctuary, or community. But what was that environment of Olive Hill, in cultural and horticultural terms?

Before the Spanish arrived, there were isolated settlements of Native Americans in the region. In 1781, the Pueblo de Los Angeles was founded about eight miles to the south of Olive Hill. Within ten years, the small pueblo had become an agricultural center, green and moist in winter, dusty and dry in summer. In 1802 Olive Hill formed part of the rancho of 6,647 acres granted to Josef Vicente Feliz. With the gold rush of 1848, people streamed into northern and central parts of California, but Southern California remained relatively isolated for some time, its vast landscape bounded by the Tehachapi Range and San Gabriel Mountains to the north, by deserts to the east and south, and, to the west, by the Pacific Ocean, where westerly winds and cold currents were deflected by the Channel Islands, leaving southern currents to warm the shores.[9]

Gradually the Spanish-Mexican character of Los Angeles yielded to the more entrepreneurial spirit of the rest of the United States. Water from the unreliable Los Angeles, San Gabriel and Santa Ana Rivers that drained the Los Angeles basin was supplemented by irrigation ditches. Periods of drought and flooding occurred, but the general impression made on newcomers was overwhelmingly positive: given its Mediterranean climate and some form of irrigation, the land could offer an abundance of crops (many of them introduced from Europe, including grapes and olives), a stunning range of landscapes and views, and a health-enhancing environment. By the mid-nineteenth century, Los Angeles was called the City of Vineyards.

In 1891, Southern California became "Our Italy," seen through the eyes of Charles Dudley Warner, a writer and amateur gardener from Connecticut. Warner was aware of some essential differences between Italy and Southern California, yet he focused on the similarities: ". . . some bay with its purple hills running to the blue sea, its surrounding mesas and canyons blooming in semi-tropical luxuriance, some conjunction of shore and mountain, some golden color, some white light and sharply defined shadows, some refinement of lines, some poetic tints in violet and ashy ranges, some ultramarine in the sea, or delicate blue in the sky. . . ." In Southern California, flowers and citrus fruits grew year round, winters were mild, snow touched only the distant high peaks, and a graciousness pervaded the air.[10]

By 1900, the population of this idyllic land was growing rapidly, and promoters of real estate and industry were drawing a diversity of permanent settlers: not only wintering millionaires, but also people of modest means from small towns and rural areas of the Midwest. In 1913, the Owens River Valley aqueduct began to supply the city's water needs. While Santa Barbara and Montecito became known as a haven of "hill barons," who built extensive houses reminiscent of Mediterranean villas, Los Angeles and its developing movie industry in Hollywood also began to attract people of comparable wealth and cultural aspiration.[11]

When Aline Barnsdall purchased the 36-acre Olive Hill, in June 1919, she could stand on the unplanted summit, 89 feet higher than the surrounding flatland of East Hollywood, and enjoy a 360-degree panorama of the Santa Monica Mountains, agricultural fields, incipient low-rise urban development, the Pacific Ocean, the Channel Islands, Santa Catalina Island, and the Palos Verdes Peninsula. The hill was still rural and agricultural in character, its slopes covered by more than a thousand olive trees, laid out as an orchard, with here and there a few fan palms, peppers, acacias and camphor trees. The microclimate was one of the most favorable in all of North America for growing subtropical plants: an "air-drained thermal belt," influenced mainly by the Pacific Ocean. Rain fell typically from October to March, about fourteen inches a year. The occasional hot, dry Santa Ana winds might blow down from the hills and canyons to the north, and frosts, though rare, were not unknown. However, warmer or cooler temperatures could be enjoyed in "pockets" by screening with trees, shrubs or walls, and by orienting an outdoor space to the south or north.[12]

With this promising portion of land in her possession, Barnsdall had at last a permanent foundation on which to build her dream of a community of actors and artists, drawn together to pursue their common ideals. Still restless, she would frequently revise her program and pressure her architect and contractor to get the elements designed and built quickly, while she embarked on yet another journey abroad, to "freshen her mind." She wanted a main house, secondary residences, a theatre, shops, rental housing, and perhaps a cinema. In her lifetime, some of these elements remained a dream; but those that were realized contributed materially to the vigorous social and cultural landscape yet to come. In the 1910s and 1920s, Los Angeles was, after all, still raw, lacking form and identity. But people were coming there from everywhere, the restless, the adventurous and creative ones, the misfits, and the seekers after health and natural beauty. "Los Angeles was perhaps the most highly publicized, talked about, city in the world," recalled Carey McWilliams, then a newcomer from Denver. "It was a 'now' city that piqued curiosity and interest, a city without a past. . . ."[13] In such an environment Barnsdall and Wright would be free to experiment. And both could hope to see their own landscapes of memory and imagination layered upon the site of Olive Hill.

The Client

From letters, newspaper clippings, an early twentieth-century history of American theatre, and recollections of those who knew her, Aline Barnsdall emerges as an ambitious woman, somewhat lacking in human warmth, yet idealistic, possessed by a vision. In architectural histories, she is inevitably overshadowed by Frank Lloyd Wright. If not for his stature as an architect, she might have slipped into obscurity. If not for her inconsistencies, her impatience, and what some have called vagueness, more of her vision for the flourishing of American arts on Olive Hill might have been realized. Nevertheless, in Barnsdall Park an extraordinary legacy remains, not only to be preserved by the City of Los Angeles, but now to be considered for its present and future significance, culturally and socially. In this light, the client and her vision deserve a closer look. That vision was a product of the Old World and the New World, of Europe and of California. Without the memory of the one and the prospects of the other, there would be no story of Barnsdall Park to tell.

Louisa Aline Barnsdall was the granddaughter and daughter of entrepreneurs whose fortunes were made in oil. William Barnsdall emigrated from Bedfordshire, England, to northwestern Pennsylvania in the 1830s and worked as a shoemaker until, in the late 1850s, he joined in an oil drilling venture on his brother-in-law's farm. In 1860, success in drilling drew William into partnership to build the first oil refinery. His son Theodore Newton (or T.N.), joined him while still a boy and, later, initiated drilling ventures elsewhere in northwestern Pennsylvania and further west. T.N. married in 1881 and, a year later, the first of his two daughters—Louisa Aline—was born. By 1893, the family moved to Pittsburgh, where Louisa had some schooling before embarking for Europe, to be educated in her own fashion. While father risked heavily, and usually with success, in drilling for oil and in mining for gold, silver, lead, zinc, iron and coal, daughter immersed herself in music, theatre, Europe's most romantic and sublime landscapes—Alpine mountains—and the great cities of the Old World.[1]

As a tale told by Henry James, Aline Barnsdall's story would begin here, without so much as a backward glance at the material means that allowed her entry into European circles of art and leisure. A young, affluent American woman in Europe, motherless since the death of Mrs. Barnsdall in 1907 (when Aline was 25 years old), this American princess may well have faced the classic Jamesian challenges: to live intensely and, through loss of innocence, to recognize her own nature and her social obligations to something or someone. But Aline, who must now be referred to as "Barnsdall," was perhaps too restless for James's moral vision; she declared herself a "new woman," a type relished by one of her cultural heroes, George Bernard Shaw. Too witty and ironic to be pinned down to definitions, Shaw left at least a suggestion of what this new woman might be in his *Quintessence of Ibsenism* (1891). Unlike The Womanly Woman, a composite of stereotypes cherished by traditional men, the new woman is a realist; she is wary of the institution of marriage, risks the destruction of many other sacred ideals, rejects the slavery of "duty," and, in fulfilling her own will, becomes emancipated, free.[2]

A memoir written by one of Barnsdall's former lovers, Lawrence Langner, includes a biographical sketch of Barnsdall, disguised as "Celeste": a blue-eyed creature of great enthusiasms, eager to see what lay on the other side of a mountain range—whether in the Bavarian Alps or in the American West. The two met in Berlin, in 1913; he had come on business, and she was there to study the German theatre. Both were fascinated by the stage. At the Deutsches Theater one

Aline and Betty Barnsdall, circa 1923

evening, a performance of Tolstoy's *The Living Corpse* left them both spellbound. Thereafter, "Celeste" yearned for the opportunity to present plays in this "new way" in the American theatre.[3]

The director of the Deutsches Theater was Max Reinhardt, who started Germany's first Little Theatre in a Berlin restaurant, with a series of one-act plays in an intimate setting among friends. Appointed director of the much larger Deutsches Theater in 1905, Reinhardt also transformed a nearby dance hall into a Kammerspielhaus, to produce the dramatic counterpart of chamber music. There, naturalistic dramas of Ibsen, Shaw, Wolf, and Strindberg, and poetic dramas of Maeterlinck, Goethe, and others were staged in settings that were considered "austerely lovely." And decorative dramas, exotic and brilliantly colorful—so unlike the more emotionally charged, romantic drama of the past—were presented simply for the sake of beauty.[4]

Dreaming of becoming an actress, Barnsdall studied for about a year with Eleonora Duse before the actress suggested a role better suited to Barnsdall's talents—that of judging and, given her means, producing plays.[5] Barnsdall was apparently dismayed, but in the writings of Edward Gordon Craig she found more than consolation. Craig (who had worked with Duse, Isadora Duncan, and other great talents) proposed that the artistic achievement of a theatrical production was, properly, due to one figure above all—not the actor, nor the playwright, but the director/producer, someone of great vision, ideally an artist experienced in all the crafts of the theatre: writing, acting, and designing and making the costumes, sets, and lighting arrangements.[6]

Craig was one exemplar of the aesthetic movement who worked with Max Reinhardt in Berlin, with Constantin Stanislavsky at the Moscow Art Theatre, and with William Butler Yeats at the Abbey Theatre, in Dublin. The son of the great actress Ellen Terry, Craig played minor roles in the shadow of Henry Irving between 1889 and 1897 before leaving acting altogether for a lifetime of inquiry into the aesthetic aspects of theatre, working as a set designer, lighting designer, critic and educator. His sets, considered remarkable for their broad masses of solid color, simplified form, and evocative lighting of background screens, were only faintly suggested in his conceptual sketches. As reproduced in black and white, these are like pale shadows of, say, Otto Wagner's Vienna Postal Savings Bank interiors, of 1905-1906, or Giorgio De Chirico's urban scenes, strange, silent and surreal, painted a few years later.[7]

To achieve Craig's ideal—a single, powerful impression—acting would have to become more stylized and less intensely personal, and the writing of plays would become less "literary." Plain language would be imbued with symbolism and the sense of mystery or ritual. None of these qualities would appeal immediately to the broad public of that time; hence the need for small experimental theatres, something like an artist's workshop, where individual egos would be subsumed in the greater work of the serene, noncommercial, spiritually enriching whole. Craig's views, published from 1905 onward, were once considered "the most revolutionary ideas that have come to our theatre since Ibsen."[8] Yeats admired the man's genius, yet he grew to be wary of Craig's difficult temperament and vagueness.[9] Craig did not aim for precision or theory, however; he meant to offer suggestions for a renewal of dignity, simplicity, and austerity in the theatre, qualities that he traced to ancient Greek Drama and the arts of the Orient, including the Japanese Noh theatre.

Barnsdall may have met Craig at his educational center, the School for the Art of the Theatre, which he and his associates established in 1912, at the Arena Goldoni, in Florence.[10] Or perhaps they first met in England, where Barnsdall is said to have studied with Craig.[11] In any event, conservative friends of Barnsdall had reservations about her reading Craig's works "with many thrills and not much understanding."[12] These friends could hardly be counted on to share Barnsdall's sympathies with political revolutionaries and radical social causes. But she was shaping her own paths. Like the regal heroine of Yeats's play, *The Shadowy Waters* (1894-1906), which Barnsdall would produce in Los Angeles in 1916-1917, this American abroad would remain fearless, at home only on uncharted seas.[13]

When Barnsdall returned to the United States in the summer of 1913, the Little Theatre movement had just reached America; the 1911-1912 season had opened with three new theatres of this type, in New York, Boston, and Chicago.[14] In New York, Langner happened to tell Barnsdall about a small art theatre in Chicago, directed by Maurice Browne. And with that, unable to find spiritual breathing space in New York, Barnsdall abruptly moved to Chicago, where she met Browne (an Englishman) and his American wife Ellen Van Volkenburgh. Soon, with co-director Arthur Bissell, Barnsdall found space for her new Players Producing Company in the building then housing Browne's tiny 99-seat theatre—the Fine Arts Building (next door to Adler and Sullivan's Auditorium Building) on South Michigan Avenue. There, in 1914-1915, she and Bissell produced four plays, one of which traveled to New York, where it was a critical success.[15]

During this season, Barnsdall offered to finance the building of a larger theatre for her neighbors, Browne and Van Volkenburgh. Sometime around the end of 1914, the journalist Henry Blackman Sell introduced her to Frank Lloyd Wright. And Barnsdall became convinced that the architect for the theatre had to be Wright. Their long, difficult yet productive relationship will be considered below. Here, a few questions should briefly be raised. Why was Barnsdall so determined to engage Wright? And why begin by commissioning a building for a rival company—a commission that would, in less than a year, be redefined as a theatre community and home for Barnsdall herself?

Barnsdall considered Wright the finest architect in the United States.[16] She may have seen his work in the folios and monograph published by Wasmuth in Berlin, in 1911. Of course, she would have seen evidence of Wright's abilities, daily, in the Fine Arts building, in the shops and galleries that he had designed there for other clients. Buildings Wright had designed stood out from their surroundings on the streets of urban and suburban Chicago. The older, domestic work was more horizontally spreading and private than the neighboring houses, while the newest, most recently celebrated work, the Midway Gardens, was extraordinary: an elaborate restaurant and cafe/beer garden, mysterious and romantic, that integrated painting and sculpture with architecture and gardening.

Wright had also done working drawings for Adler and Sullivan's theatres, notably the one in the Auditorium Building (1886-1890), known for its exceptional acoustics.[17] Moreover, Wright's own work revealed aesthetic qualities that Barnsdall had learned to value in the Little Theatre stage sets of Berlin, London, and elsewhere: in the restraint, austerity, abstraction, and strangely haunting, archaic quality of broad masses, solid colors, and stylization—akin to works of ancient Egypt, Greece, and the living traditions of the Orient, especially Japan. Beyond these affinities to works remote in time and place, Wright's interiors also encouraged a fresh, liberating experience of space. In prairie house, temple, and office building, the architectural "box" had been broken, opened up, and Barnsdall may have hoped for a similar spatial experience in the theatre as well.

Barnsdall may have wished to finance a theatre for Browne because it seemed a risk worth taking; it could bring financial rewards, and the artistic quality of his productions would be in itself rewarding. But soon Barnsdall wanted her own theatre. She wanted to produce plays of her own choosing, in a theatre designed by an architect she chose, working with her choice of actors, directors, and staff. This theatre would offer scope for her artistic sensibilities without demanding of her the supreme sacrifice that Craig had insisted a true artist, a perfectionist, must make: to live for an ideal, and for the sake of that ideal, to see everything else in the world destroyed.[18] He saw his own role not precisely as an artist, but as someone with both artistic vision and a head for business. Barnsdall, too, must have assumed some such role. But, whereas Craig tried for some time to maintain the aesthetic movement's ideal of art for art's sake, Barnsdall could not make that commitment. She appears to have been more persuaded by Shaw, in whose essays and plays she would have heard echoes of Fabian socialism, a movement committed to the reform of the entire, imperfect social and economic organization of that time.[19] Uncommitted, Barnsdall nevertheless remained intrigued by the possibilities for both art and social reform.

What Barnsdall retained from reading Shaw was not only a keen sense of her will to be free, but also the critical role that the arts had played in her own life, sharpening her awareness of the world and thus her ability to be free. Something of this awareness and appreciation she wanted to extend to others, especially through theatre. What she learned from Craig may have been somewhat vague, but it ranged from the aesthetic to the pragmatic.

So much for the lessons of the Old World. Now the New World beckoned, and, for Barnsdall as for countless others, the most powerful attraction lay westward, in the land not yet developed, not yet shaped by many layers of cultivation, yet already mythical in its broad appeal for the adventurous and the fearless, the entrepreneur and the visionary. In California, in the decades before the first world war, new political, social, educational and artistic ideas were nurtured in environments that were not yet institutionalized. Populism, feminism, Fabian socialism, a Christian Socialist Economic League (in Los Angeles), the kindergarten movement, a literary magazine, *Land of Sunshine* (which later became *Out West*), and other manifestations of a reforming or redefining spirit had already created their own audiences and adherents.[20] For Barnsdall, the appeal must have been irresistible. Having tried to realize her dreams of a new American theatre in New York and Chicago, Barnsdall returned from a visit to the Golden State convinced that her path lay westward. "If the theatre is to again become a great force in the world," she remarked to Wright and Norman Bel Geddes, in 1916, "it is going to happen here in America where we have freedom of thought and action. And that, too, is why my theatre must be in California rather than in New York."[21]

The attempts to realize Barnsdall's dream of an American theatre can now be taken up from the architect's point of view. Looking back many years later, Wright recalled that he had approached the project as a holiday adventure, a meeting of Circumstance and Opportunity, in a most appealing land. He wrote, "Miss Aline Barnsdall turned this beautiful site, Olive Hill, over to me as a basis on which we were to go work *together* to build under the serene blue canopy of California."[22] As it happened, they were rarely together in space and time; they communicated mainly by telegraph.

The Architect

Frank Lloyd Wright never seems to be more at peace with himself than when he writes of the land. In his memory, even the hardships associated with his boyhood on the farm in Wisconsin—weeding, hoeing, chopping, getting the cows out of the corn, and struggling with the brightly colored, dangerous machines—all fed the life of his imagination, as did countless small, precise details in the landscape. The stones among the dew-laden grasses somehow didn't cut his bare feet as, too tired to sleep, he would slip out of his bed to wander in the moonlight. Climbing a ridge, he would look out over fertile valleys and begin to make out patterns that emerged from the darkness, patterns of trees that changed, depending on whether the moon shone *on* them or *against* them. Flowers, deprived of their colors, glistened like pale gems. Shadows were deep, mysterious, and the mists were horizontal: "Broad, shallow mists, distilled from heavy dews, floating in cool, broad sheets below were lying free over the treetops in long, thin, flat ribands." The quiet was broken only by the drone of insects. "The ancient element of moisture seemed to prevail there as a kind of light flooding over all."[1]

In the same expansive spirit Wright wrote of his home at Taliesin, which was built overlooking the same ancestral valley, land of his mother's people. Named for an ancient Welsh poet, literally "shining brow," Taliesin was constructed on the brow of a gentle hill—not on its summit. For Wright, it was meant to be a home, an architect's workshop, a farm, and a self-sustaining community. Stone for the structure would be quarried nearby, and the house, a *natural* house, would belong to its hill as the trees and rock ledges belonged there.

This story, now a legend, often omits the architect's vision of Taliesin before any building began: the crown of the hill as a single mass of apple trees in bloom, its fragrance drifting down the valley; snow-white plums, ruby-like currants, and vineyards heavy with purple, green and yellow grapes; melons, bees, a herd of cattle, Javanese peacocks, and other impressions of sight, sound, smell, and taste. In the surrounding hills and valleys Wright saw patterns for the buildings that would follow: "The lines of the hills were the lines of the roofs, the slopes of the hills their slopes, the plastered surfaces of the light wood-walls, set back into shade beneath the broad eaves, were like the flat stretches of sand in the river below and the same in color. . . ." Stone, wood, and sand for plaster would be in harmony with the land, all woven together such that it would be hard to tell where pavement left off and ground began, or where walls left off and gardens began.[2]

This vision of natural, or organic, architecture lay behind his maxim, "The land is the simplest form of architecture."[3] Or, as the Taliesin fellowship often heard Wright say, "The land is the beginning of architecture."[4] Ideally, any new project would begin with a broad understanding of the land. Later would come architecture: "man in possession of his earth."[5]

Despite his tone of serenity, Wright had no illusions about the absolute tranquility of the land; it was formed by cosmic elements—heat, glaciers, winds, waters—that had been at work since the first cataclysms of creation. Stone, the basic material of the planet, had its origins in violence. "All is scarred by warring forces seeking reconciliation, still marred by conflict and conquest," he wrote. "Ceaselessly, the rock masses are made by fire, are laid low by water, are sculptured by wind and stream."[6] These changes took place slowly, over geologic eras. But acts of violence could still occur in nature with no more warning than the violence that

Frank Lloyd Wright, circa 1930

struck Taliesin, in August, 1914, just a short time before Wright met Aline Barnsdall. The multiple murders committed by his deranged servant, followed by the near consumption of Taliesin by fire, would have shattered a person less determined to live and create. But Wright emerged from darkness, determined to rebuild on that land (which he did, twice in his lifetime). Thereafter, in moments of conflict, Wright would assume a task that had cosmic overtones: to bring harmony (or order) out of chaos.

The conflicts that developed around Barnsdall's relations with Wright and her many requests for designs, renderings and models, have been carefully traced by Kathryn Smith, whose research forms the basis of the following account (much abbreviated).[7] Here, beginning with Barnsdall's first impulse to build in Chicago, we trace the main lines of Wright's development of the *land* of Olive Hill: how he perceived it, altered it, and invested it with new layers of meaning. The contributions of Lloyd Wright and R.M. Schindler will be noted, briefly, along with a few of Barnsdall's own reservations.

In 1915, Barnsdall asked Wright to design a theatre, to be built in Chicago for the artistic productions of Maurice Browne and Ellen Van Volkenburgh. Wright's design, including plans, sections, and front elevation for the 450-seat theatre, with one or two stories for studios, was square in plan. A great circle within generated the form of stage and seating. Clearly an *urban* project, it suggested no relationship to any context beyond its front entrance on the street. That year, Barnsdall traveled to California and returned to Chicago with plans to settle in San Francisco, establish a theatre company there, and take a few plays on tour to New York City and along the California coast. If she were successful, she would then build her own theatre.

Barnsdall left for California in February, 1916, just about the time when the manager of the old Imperial Hotel in Tokyo arrived at Taliesin to discuss Wright's plans for a new hotel (a potential commission dating from 1913). By the summer of 1916, Barnsdall was disappointed by the dim prospects for a small independent theatre in San Francisco. Waiting for her father's approval to proceed, she wrote to Wright, reiterating her request for a building with studios, something with "the grace of the Midway Gardens."[8] That summer she moved to Los Angeles, where her Players Producing Company staged six plays during the 1916-1917 season, with artistic direction by Richard Ordynski and set designs by Norman Bel Geddes. By the beginning of 1917, Wright was in Tokyo, working on the Imperial Hotel. In February, Barnsdall's father died. At the end of the 1917 season, Barnsdall dissolved her company. Later in the year she gave birth to a child, whose father was believed to be the former artistic director, Ordynski. Barnsdall remained unmarried and attended to her child and her father's estate.

Wright's work in Tokyo, Barnsdall's preoccupation with legal entanglements of the estate, and her indecision over her future as a theatrical producer all contributed to delays. In January, 1918, she encouraged Wright to proceed with plans for a larger theatre, eliminating the studios. While a site had not yet been purchased, Wright altered his designs, increasing the theatre's seating from 450 to 1,500, and made several changes to bring actors and spectators into a closer spatial relationship. There was some discussion of Wright's designing a house for Barnsdall. He repeatedly asked for more time, while Barnsdall, with neither a site nor a city determined, kept asking for more specific designs.

By the time Barnsdall purchased Olive Hill, in June, 1919, Wright's design for Hollyhock House was remarkably suggestive of the house as now built: an axial and cross-axial scheme of building masses and courtyards, with a weaving of building and landscape that apparently drew on the precedents of Taliesin, several of Wright's Prairie houses, Mayan temples and the prints of Hokusai, with an elegant suggestion of Mt. Fuji rising behind the mountain- or mesa-like masses of the house. In one lovely bird's eye view, what appears to be a woodland of Lombardy poplars or Italian cypress is bisected by a straight path on axis with the central mass (the living room) and its square reflecting pool: a dreamlike, faint suggestion of some Italian villa, with walled gardens and groves, overlaid with a fragment of Wright's Avery Coonley House, in Riverside, Illinois.[9] The gardens are not truly walled in, however, and the monumental building masses seem somehow to float. What matters, here, is not the guessing game of precedents. Rather, in the absence of a determined site, Wright was free to consider his work a "romanza," a free-form composition relying on memory and a sense of proportion. Playing with ornament—a stylized hollyhock—he would take a "holiday" from his self-imposed task of expressing the materials and machines of his day.[10] He would also be on holiday in that particular landscape, treating it not with the filial affection he had shown in the Mid-West, but with a freer spirit of adventure.

There is a possibility that Wright had visited the site sometime *before* he appeared there in September, 1919, straight from Japan, via Seattle.[11] This may never be verified, but one thing is clear: whenever he did first visit the site, Wright was profoundly affected. The scale of the larger landscape was vast, and the views towards mountains and plain, ocean and islands, were exhilarating. For anyone born east of the Rocky Mountains, that first experience of the scale, the sweep, and the drama of unbuilt, unspoiled Southern California in those years could be both liberating and unsettling. For the mature architect of "prairie" houses, one's accomplished manner of imitating the local rock ledges and trees was no longer relevant. The old, familiar sense of *belonging* to a particular landscape, nestling into the brow of a hill so as to gaze down upon one's own little ancestral valley, all that was now beyond reach. Olive Hill, even with thirty years' growth of an orchard, was still part wilderness, untamed, awaiting the refinement of gardens, groves and human shelter, yet resistant to any adaptation of an old, familiar style or way of life. And so this strange Southern California wilderness, punctuated here and there by a Hollywood version of ancient Babylon or a fairy castle, challenged Wright to dig deeper into a mythical, pre-Columbian and even geological past, to begin to understand the spirit of the place, then to evoke it in shaped spaces, beneath or beyond a sheltering roof.

In previous years, people used to congregate on the unplanted summit of Olive Hill for Easter sunrise services. Barnsdall had explained to the press that she meant to keep Olive Hill's stunning views accessible to the public, and would open up her own gardens as well; nevertheless she asked Wright to place her house on the crown of the hill. Doing so would, of course, forever change one's experience of the summit and its views outward. Wright acquiesced.

His first master plan, of 1919, drawn in pencil over a topographic map of Olive Hill, retained the existing grove roads that followed the contours as they rose from the semi-circular drive at the northeast corner of the site. Wright also retained the existing grid of olive trees, planted 20 feet on center. Where the planting had deviated from this grid on the periphery, he regularized it and, in effect, extended the grid to generate the axes of his plan.

Barnsdall House, circa 1916-1918

For the main house on the summit, he established an east/west main axis and a north/south cross-axis. Over time, Wright would shift the precise location of axes and structures, while maintaining the same orientation of views: from the living room westward, to the Pacific; and, from the music room northward, along the palm-lined Berendo Street toward a peak of the Hollywood Hills. East of Hollyhock House would be a grove of tall trees, effective as a verdant background, as a screen from the theatre, and as an element that added stature to the hill, seen from below. While structures were added or eliminated over time, some harmony was maintained by the strong geometry—the grid—laid over the irregular topography.

In several pencil and ink wash drawings dating from 1919 or earlier, some individual structures, particularly the theatre, appear as sculptural objects against the dense foliage of silvery green olives, backed by darker, denser masses of pines. Less apparent in these drawings was Wright's growing feeling for interior space as the very essence of architecture, space to be experienced as continuum. At Olive Hill, the sense of an "interior landscape," expanding and flowing outward, is most apparently in Hollyhock House, its courts and its gardens. Something of this weaving of land and buildings can be traced to Wright's beloved Taliesin, but there is also a strong evocation of the villa.

Before Taliesin was even conceived, Wright had spent the winter and spring of 1909-1910 in Europe. With the help of his son Lloyd and another draftsman, Taylor Wolley, he was preparing the final drawings of his work, to be published by Wasmuth, in Berlin. But he was also getting to know the villas of Italy, particularly those in and around Fiesole, including the Villa Medici.[12] In the company of his lover Mamah Cheney or with his son Lloyd, Wright would explore the secret gardens, sunny terraces, shadowy groves and staircases of Italian villas. Later he would recall details of the tiny hillside villa that he and Mamah had shared in Fiesole: the high-walled garden, a little garden by the pool, an arbor of climbing yellow roses, a small fountain, and a small stone table covered with a white cloth, set for two. In his memory were mingled the pleasures of the table, the romance of the gardens, the fields full of poppies, the odor of great pines, the song of the nightingale, the shadows and the moonlight.[13] Perhaps inevitably, the Mediterranean climate of Southern California or some particular evocation of Italy on Olive Hill would stir such memories.

One indispensable element of the Italian villa was water: flowing, spraying or still; invested with pagan, Christian, or intensely personal symbolism; employed to connect a series of gardens, to cool a bottle of wine, or to mirror the sky. On Olive Hill, Wright also explored the uses of water as he linked his architecture with its site, both visually and symbolically. In the plan of 1919, the "spring house," near the southeast corner of the retaining wall of Hollyhock House, is one source. From there, a man-made stream flows south and southeast, winding its way toward, around and below the director's house, and on to a calm, naturalistic lake at the base of Olive Hill. As Wright's various schemes were refined, an idea which he later realized more dramatically at Fallingwater was anticipated on Olive Hill: that of integrating a flowing stream, symbolic of life and energy, with a home. In the plan of 1919, only the director's house is truly integrated with this stream; and Smith interprets this with the idea that the director's house is truly the *center* of the creative imagination, as well as the pulsating heart of the community. With some poetic justice, perhaps Wright designed this feature anticipating that he himself might live there, as Barnsdall suggested, while he completed his designs for the theatre.

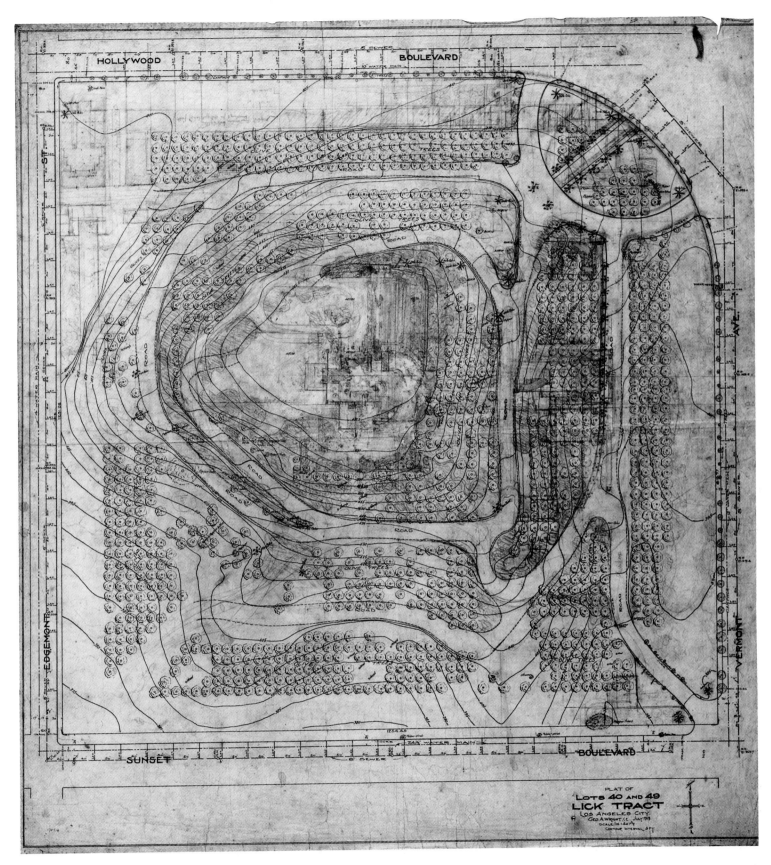

Topographic map and first plan of Olive Hill, 1919

In the second master plan, of 1920, Wright added several structures at Barnsdall's request, including two residences, a movie theatre, a row of shops, and a revised watercourse. Taking its source closer to Hollyhock House and avoiding the Director's house, this water flows into a larger lake along Vermont Avenue. In the next few years, overlaid on this plan were the site of a children's school, or Community Playhouse (which Wright nicknamed "Little Dipper"), and some commercial sites. This was a time when Lloyd Wright made substantial contributions to the landscape design, supervising the construction of buildings, roads and water elements from about December, 1919, to August, 1920. He also made several perspective drawings for Hollyhock House and prepared a General Planting Plan, along with detailed planting designs. Schindler, having worked in Wright's office from 1918 to 1922, opened his own office in West Hollywood in September, 1922. In 1924 he designed a terrace with wading pool, pergola, a garden and a fountain on the site originally intended for Wright's "Little Dipper" playhouse. For this terrace. Richard Neutra executed perspective drawings and designed the landscape.[14]

On Olive Hill, Wright, Lloyd Wright, Schindler and Neutra, all architects with exceptional talents for integrating structures with the land, were given a marvelous site for creating gardens. The potential uses of these gardens would challenge any designer's imagination: parties, concerts, theatrical performances, strolling, contemplation, even exploration and discovery—the expansion of a child's imagination. And these architects cared about gardens! Schindler and Neutra, both born and educated in Vienna, grew up in a city of superb gardens. Lloyd Wright had studied gardens and landscape design; with his father and with Taylor Wolley, he had toured gardens in Europe, and he had worked as a draftsman for Olmsted and Olmsted in Boston and San Diego.[15] Ironically, what Lloyd and his colleagues created on the land—the very essence—of Olive Hill was the most fragile and ephemeral of all.

For a while, Barnsdall was keenly interested in the gardens, their color schemes, and the species of their trees and plants. She cared about her theatre, her child's development, and her incipient community on the hill. But she became distanced by her frequent journeys abroad, her indecision, and her strained relations with Wright (which he traced to the contractor and advisors, who formed a barrier between client and architect). Ultimately he was unable to satisfy Barnsdall's demands for economy and speed. With the threat of lawsuits pending from both sides, Wright and Barnsdall ended their working relationship (and his contract) in December, 1923. Years later, however, with improved relations, they remained friends.[16]

When the higher ground of Olive Hill became Barnsdall Park, the land and structures began to accommodate new meanings along with new purposes (considered below, in the 1995 Master Plan). But was there ever an intrinsic meaning, shared by both architect and client, in the designs for Olive Hill? One can only speculate. Before leaving his temporary home on this site, for instance, Wright wrote a brochure, *Experimenting with Human Lives* (1923), in which he reflected on the geological processes of "seismic convulsions," or earthquakes, known to occur along the rim of the basin of the Pacific Ocean. He recalled the sacred Mount Fujiyama, brooding in majesty and beauty over the scenes of occasional terror, when the same forces that created the mountain begin to strain, crack the earth's crust, and yield to flames. Neil Levine finds in these reflections Wright's tendency to idealize the forces of nature; and he suggests that Hollyhock House is itself a microcosm of the Los Angeles basin, with its mesa-like building masses and its watercourse flowing from circular pool, to meandering streams in the courtyard, to square reflecting pool.

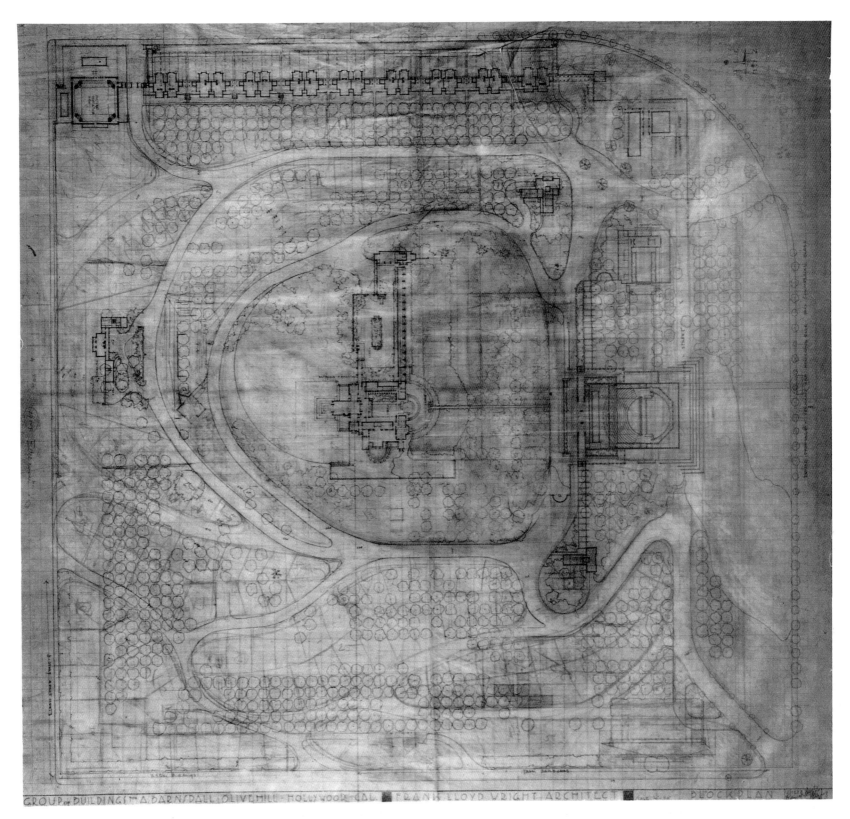

GROUP of BUILDINGS A. BARNSDALL · OLIVE HILL · HOLLYWOOD · CAL ■ FRANK LLOYD WRIGHT ARCHITECT ■ BLOCK PLAN

Olive Hill plan with the addition of several structures, 1920

Along the way, this watercourse emerges from underground into the living room, where it fills a trough around the fireplace. Above the hearth, illuminated by a great skylight, is a stylized pictograph that seems to resist a single interpretation. One meaning was offered by Lloyd Wright: it depicts Aline Barnsdall as an Indian princess, seated on her throne, looking out over her desert mesas.[17] Around her are the four primordial elements: earth, air, fire, and water.

If these interpretations are valid, then a certain irony remains. Much as she admired Native Americans and their culture, Barnsdall did not develop an attachment for the house in which a stylized Indian princess was inscribed in her honor. Wright offered Barnsdall nothing less than a dramatic, monumental house that commanded its site with a hint of royalty. This house had its own watercourse, apparently independent from that which Wright would have liked to provide for the artistic director of the proposed theater. Barnsdall could reign in splendor on the summit, while the artistic director, housed in a site of slightly lower elevation, could remain in more intimate contact with nature, the source of the inspiration needed to direct a community of artists of the theatre. But this solution could not have satisfied Barnsdall for long.

Barnsdall's colleagues in the theatre remembered her as indecisive, unable to give a true sense of direction. And yet she craved a degree of authority; to Bel Geddes she wrote, "The organization of the company, its standard, choice of plays, decorators, actors, etc. must be my personal expression—the thing on which I stand or fall."[18] She did not want to be a figurehead. She believed she had more to offer than money and a head for business, yet she was not an artist committed to art above all else. Fond of travel, her studies, and the outdoors, and devoted to her child, she was looking for some sort of Arcadia in the United States. Wright nearly offered her just that, with a house and grounds somewhat too monumental, too theatrical, for her personal needs. As she had explained to a journalist, "I seem forced to try, at least, to create a domicile fitting for the art which is, I believe, destined to help form the taste and ideals of the world. . . ."[19] In these aims, with the help of her architect, Barnsdall largely succeeded. Barnsdall Park, on Olive Hall, remains her gift to later generations, as durable as the determination of the people of Los Angeles to maintain her home, gardens, grounds, structures, and artistic vision.

If Wright is to have a final word about meaning, let it be resonant. Writing of some of the greatest civilizations on earth, including the Mayan, Egyptian, Greek, Persian, Chinese and Japanese, Wright found in their architecture a common origin in human nature, the *human spirit*. Over time, the physical matter of their ancient buildings lay in ruins, comparable, in Wright's view, to geological deposits washed up by ancient seas. The value of these ancient ruins, for later generations, would lie in the recognition of the human spirit that had conceived them. Some pattern of abstract form might be recognized in the ruins; but it could not be too closely imitated, for the human spirit that had first conceived and breathed life into those buildings was gone. Pattern was an abstraction, a clue. What will be man's essential pattern in our time? Wright asked. His response was a new ideal—organic architecture—and a new emphasis on interior space, a new sense of spatial continuity, to bring order out of chaos. "The old—'classic,' eclecticism—is chaos, restlessness," he wrote in 1937. "The new—'integral,' organic—is order, repose."[20]

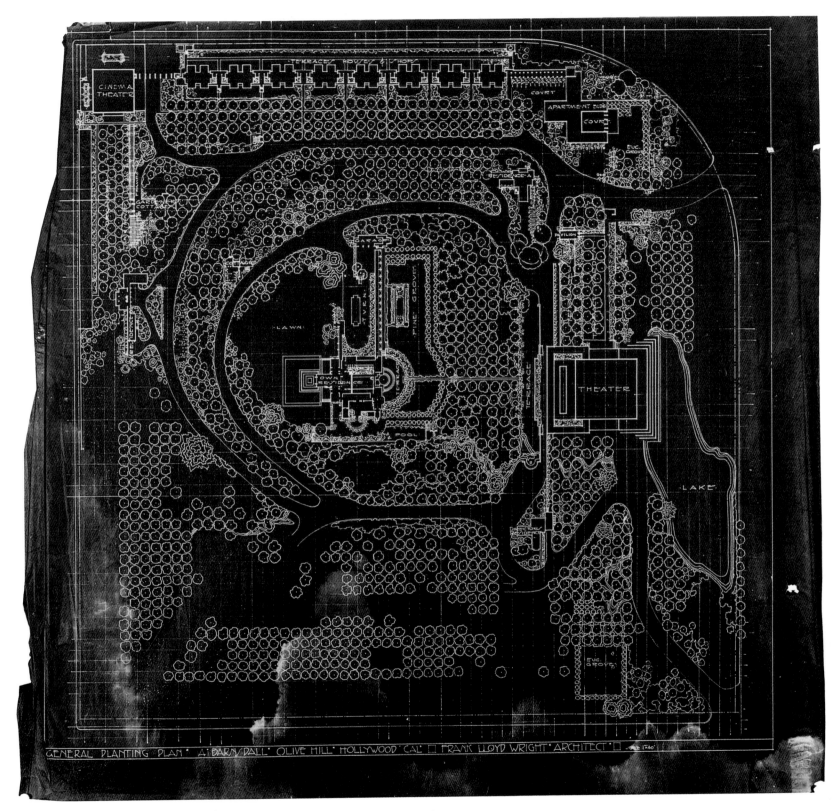

General planting plan for Olive Hill, 1920, which retains the original grid of olive trees, 20 feet on center

The Master Plan

Nearly sixty years after the publication of Wright's views on ancient civilizations and organic architecture, quoted above, a new master plan for Barnsdall Park is now up for review. It, too, seeks a measure of order and repose. It, too, looks for essential patterns, based on several previous master plans, detailed plans, renderings, period photographs and other evidence of the designers' intentions. What this master plan does *not* attempt, however, is to focus on individual buildings. It goes beyond architectural preservation to encompass the historic preservation of gardens, groves, orchards, structures, paths, roads, and their relationships. It focuses on the land: a physical place that has historic cultural value, locally, nationally and internationally.

Perhaps the closest counterparts to Barnsdall Park in cultural terms would be the communities that were designed, or adapted, for a range of educational, artistic and cultural pursuits: the American and French academies in Rome, for example; the Villa I Tatti, near Florence; Cranbrook, in Bloomfield Hills, Michigan; and other memorable places, where the experience of landscape is an inseparable part of one's total experience. What distinguishes Barnsdall Park from other favored places of cultivation and creativity, however, is the accommodation made for commercial space and rental housing on the original site. This mix of uses, which Barnsdall requested early on, compelled Wright to act as an urban designer, not for some imaginary situation such as he would later assume for his Broadacre City prototypes, but for an actual city, living and growing.

Hence the need for conservation, not simply preservation. Rather than strive for a museum-like atmosphere, a place "frozen" at one particular point in its development, the master plan accounts for the kinds of flux and change that all living communities experience. It remains open to, even encourages, some developments that cannot be foreseen in detail. Strategic guidelines, for instance, are offered for dealing with the sensitive edges—the areas where the Park and its immediate neighbors, commercial and institutional, share common interests and views outward or inward. These guidelines are meant not only to minimize negative impacts but also to set up positive, creative interaction between the park and its urban neighbors. Funding and implementation strategies are also offered in this spirit of cooperation. Essentially, this master plan is realistic and pragmatic, given the current urban situation of East Hollywood and its region of Los Angeles. The plan proposes a series of intelligent choices to be made. In the balance lie two equally desirable and not necessarily opposing values: history, or memory; and vitality, along with the unpredictable aspects of change.

Historic Value

Barnsdall Park is the only landscape designed by Frank Lloyd Wright and his son Lloyd Wright that is currently used as a city-owned public park. It may also be the most complete example of Wright's talents in the design of the land. For these reasons alone the park is an historic resource of international significance. The need for conserving this legacy, for restoring and repairing the elements of its landscape, should be self-evident. But there is another reason for landscape preservation. Aline Barnsdall's gift of the park, formally accepted by the City in January, 1927, was made with the stipulation that Hollyhock House and any future

Olive Hill, 1947

buildings in the park must be used as facilities for art and artistic activities, in perpetuity. Historically, these activities have included performances in the buildings and courtyards; in a variety of ways, then, the experience of the landscape has often entered into one's experience of the visual and performing arts at Barnsdall Park. On some level, perhaps unconscious for some, the land is the beginning of that experience.

Concern for both accuracy of historic detail and the elusive "spirit of the place" led the planners to pay close attention to the Historic Site Survey of Barnsdall Park, completed in June, 1995. This survey makes the site real: a physical landscape shaped as a community, not merely a collection of buildings. And what changes it reveals! The rural vision of Olive Hill in 1919 gives way, in 1920, to an apparent differentiation between two zones: incipient urbanism at the base of the hill and, above, an emerging acropolis, cultivated, urbane, somewhat remote. In turn, the gentle weaving of buildings and landscape first realized at Taliesin has been left far behind in Wright's last master plan for Barnsdall Park, of 1958-59. Here, curving drives, streamlined underpasses, an elegant pool, and an art gallery and administration center (with a tall, slim tower) recall the dynamism of Wright's Marin County Civic Center, designed at about the same time, for a hilly site in Northern California. Apart from its visual appeal as a vintage "landscape for the motor age," this effort on Wright's part to accommodate the desires of the current generation at Barnsdall park, even to overlay a futuristic landscape over a portion of his own earlier landscape design, sets a precedent. It implies that any subsequent master plan may be respectful of the past and yet inventive, hopeful, cheerful.

The 1995 master plan accepts as a given the general principles stated in November, 1991, by the Planning and Development Committee of the Barnsdall Park Board of Overseers. The advancement and enjoyment of the arts will remain the focus of the park, while a range of activities, from arts events to passive recreation, will be encouraged. The topography and the experience of open space on Olive Hill are essential to the park. Any new projects in the park must be considered in light of the park's historical significance. The park must become more accessible, visually and physically; views should be preserved and enhanced. The character of the edges—the areas where the park and the neighboring properties meet—should be improved with consideration for the views out from, and into, these areas. Finally, the Park's Board of Overseers, composed of representatives from the City, the neighborhoods, and the institutional and commercial buildings around the park, should review all proposals that might have some bearing on the development of the park and its environs.

The Historic Site Survey, a product of this 1991 planning vision, calls for reinforcing five characteristics of Barnsdall Park, in order to maintain the essence of its historical character: topography, views and access, historical structures, landscape character, and paths and roads. These characteristics suggested a point of departure for the new Master Plan. Also important in shaping the new plan were considerations that reflect present and future realities: the concerns of people who live and work near the park, the long-range plans of the neighboring institutions and businesses, and the probable impacts of regional access to the park, once the new Metro Rail station reaches full operation. Given this wide range of issues, the Master Plan is presented as a series of opportunities, to be addressed in two phases. Phase I focuses on the renovation and enhancement of the park, while Phase II considers the park as a catalyst for creating a new, coherent urban and economic district out of formerly disconnected neighbors.

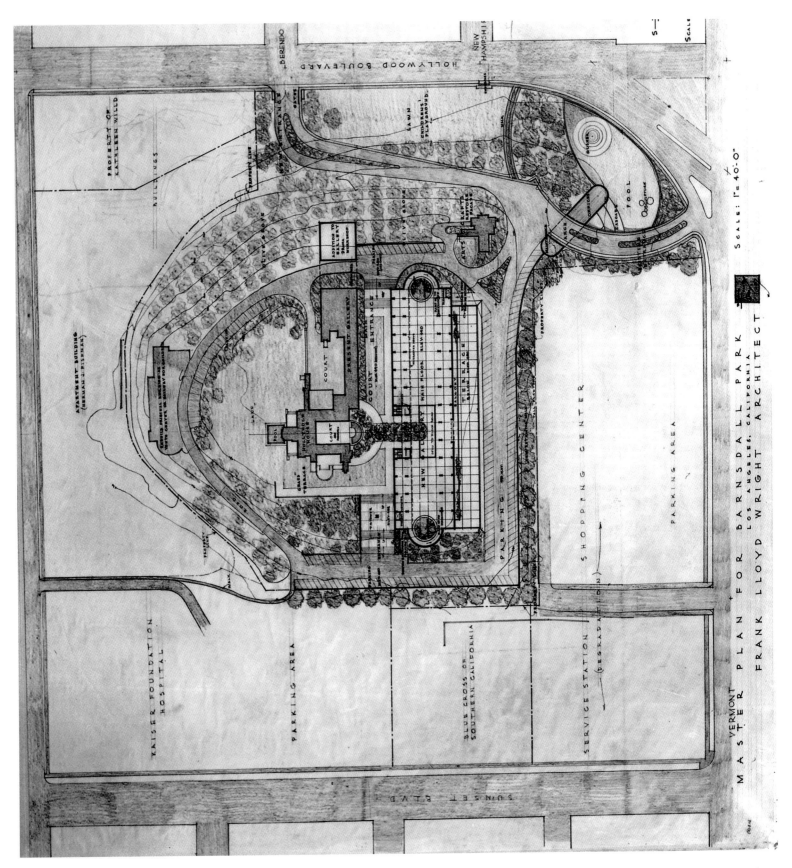

Frank Lloyd Wright's last master plan for Barnsdall Park, 1958-1959

Vitality and Change

To begin to appreciate the constraints as well as the opportunities in this planning process, let's take a look at a series of four site plans, prepared for the Historic Site Survey, that gives a synopsis of the site's vegetation and development in this century. "Olive Hill, 1919" reveals the unbuilt site with some 30 years' growth of olive orchards covering the slopes. Except for the nearly level summit and the winding access roads, the site is covered with olive trees, 1,154 in all, along with a few pepper trees and palms that line a segment of a road or punctuate a slope. Total number of trees, in 1919: 1,225.

"Barnsdall Park, 1921-46" indicates the development of the entire 36-acre property, including the 10-acre park in the center, from the first phase of construction to the death of Aline Barnsdall in December, 1946. The structures by Frank Lloyd Wright and R.M. Schindler are complemented with Lloyd Wright's and his father's additional groves of pines, gardens, and lawns near Hollyhock House; with Richard Neutra's landscape treatment of Schindler's Terrace; and with improved roads and enhanced plantings. 1,091 olive trees remain, among a richer variety of other trees, including acacias, jacarandas, willows and eucalyptus. Total number of trees in 1946: 1,829.

"Barnsdall Park, 1946-65" indicates the mixed blessings of post-war prosperity and a burgeoning population. A hospital, the medical offices, an auto agency, a car wash, and the apartments, shopping center and parking structure all represent income-producing uses of the land on the lower slopes, some of it in private hands, some held by Barnsdall's heirs. The cut-and-fill operations to accommodate these new uses change the hill's topography and destroy hundreds of trees. Within the park, Wright's exhibition pavilion, new parking areas, a new entrance road, and a new service road also contribute to the loss of trees on the original 36-acre site. Only 233 olive trees remain. Total number of trees in 1965: 445.

"Barnsdall Park, 1965-92" shows a reduced island of hilly ground rising above a sea of urban buildings and streets. As the tide of urbanism rises, the little island shrinks, becoming even more densely built. The Junior Art Center (1967), by Hunter and Benedict, with Kahn, Farrell and Associates, and the Municipal Art Gallery (1971), by Wehmueller and Stephens, are both built into the east side of Olive Hill. Below these buildings are a shopping center and a parking lot along Vermont Avenue. 90 brave olive trees remain. Total number of trees in 1992: 200.

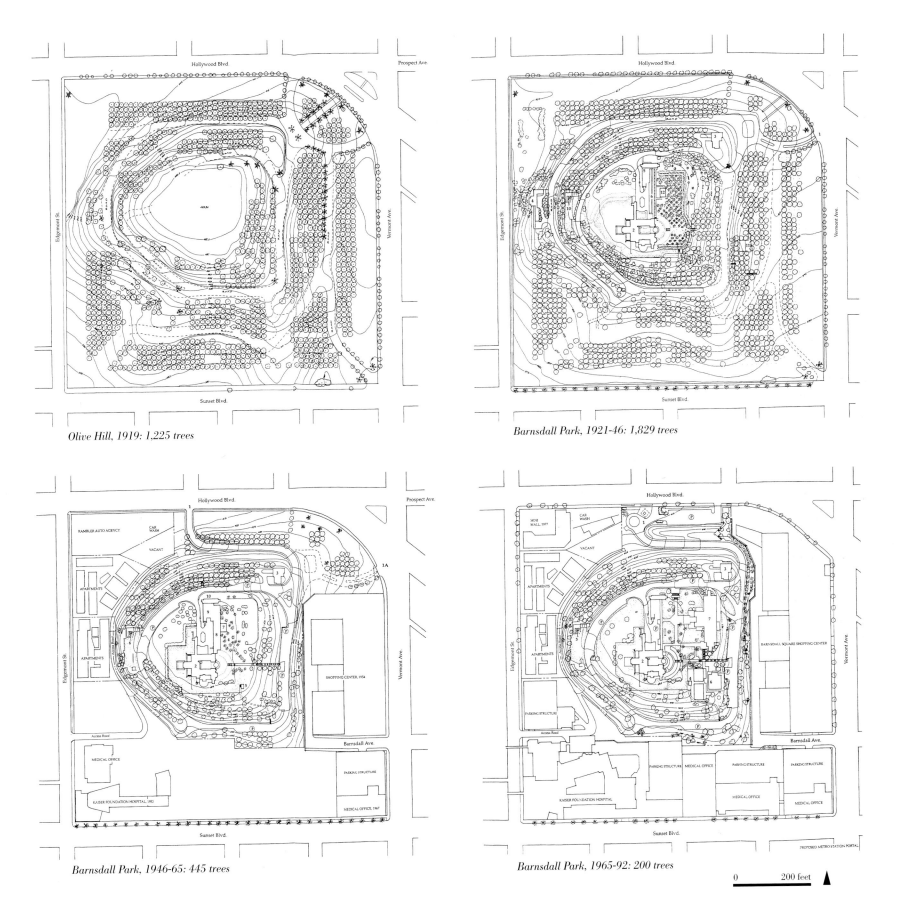

Olive Hill, 1919: 1,225 trees

Barnsdall Park, 1921-46: 1,829 trees

Barnsdall Park, 1946-65: 445 trees

Barnsdall Park, 1965-92: 200 trees

0   200 feet

The 1995 Master Plan

"Barnsdall Park Master Plan, December, 1995" is still a vision, conveyed by an elegant model, an orderly plan, a written description, and many details and artist's renderings. No longer so remote, this former island of culture and horticulture is, in many ways, reconnected to the city. The edges of city and park are no longer so distinct, as the park, with its orchard and other amenities, reaches beyond the lower slopes of Olive Hill and across the avenues and boulevards. From some demolition and some new construction, there arises a new harmony out of chaos. 1,376 olive trees cover the ground. Total number of trees proposed: 1,763.

Phase IA of this plan begins with the land, its topography, its vegetation, and its character. To evoke the spirit of Olive Hill in the 1920s, with its agricultural setting, its slower pace, and its expression of a bountiful, cultivated existence, some of the accumulations of the later decades will be removed, while some of the land itself will be regraded to assume its former aspect. Retaining walls and curbs can then be removed, and the character of the simple rural access roads can be brought back. To begin to repair the loss of more than 90% of the total number of trees on the hill, the olive orchard will be replanted in the original grid, 20 feet on center. Parking lots (which did not appear on the hill in the 1920s) will be eliminated from historically significant open spaces, and agreements with adjacent landowners will be developed, to allow overflow and event parking. In this way, more of the park itself can be experienced in a leisurely way, on foot.

Phase IB continues the replanting of olives and the rebuilding of roads, so that both may reinforce the rural character of the site. Some new trees, particularly acacias, oleanders, jacarandas and pepper trees, will be used to screen out parking lots and other less desirable sights nearby and to frame the fine distant views.

The most important innovation of this phase will be the creation of a new Arts Terrace, running north/south, halfway down the eastern slope of Olive Hill. Currently, the neighbors closest to Barnsdall Park open their front doors onto busy streets while turning their backs—their service courts and refuse cans and storage areas—toward the park. In the future, these unsightly areas will become a favored, special area: a lively terrace, with shops, restaurants, and arts-oriented facilities that face the park and share in its amenities. And, with the construction of a pedestrian and vehicular bridge connecting with the hospital's parking garage, the Arts Terrace can be further extended, inviting freer access to and from the park, particularly on occasions when the garage is made accessible to park users.

The Hilltop Gardens will be restored to their original form and character, replanted, and set off by newly regraded and replanted lawns. Views outward to Downtown Hollywood, Century City, Marina Del Rey, and the Pacific Ocean will be restored. Wright's grove of stone pines and eucalyptus trees will be replanted with a wider spacing of trees. Then, as more sunlight penetrates their canopy, the ground below can be used for classes, small gatherings and festivals. At the Motor Court of Hollyhock House, the parterres of lawn and paving will be restored to re-establish the scale of the space and entry sequence. A bookstore/cafe with moveable tables and umbrellas might be installed on the site of the original garage. (Perhaps the bookstore might specialize in topics related to Frank Lloyd Wright and the history of Los Angeles.) Other features should be brought back to their original condition and function:

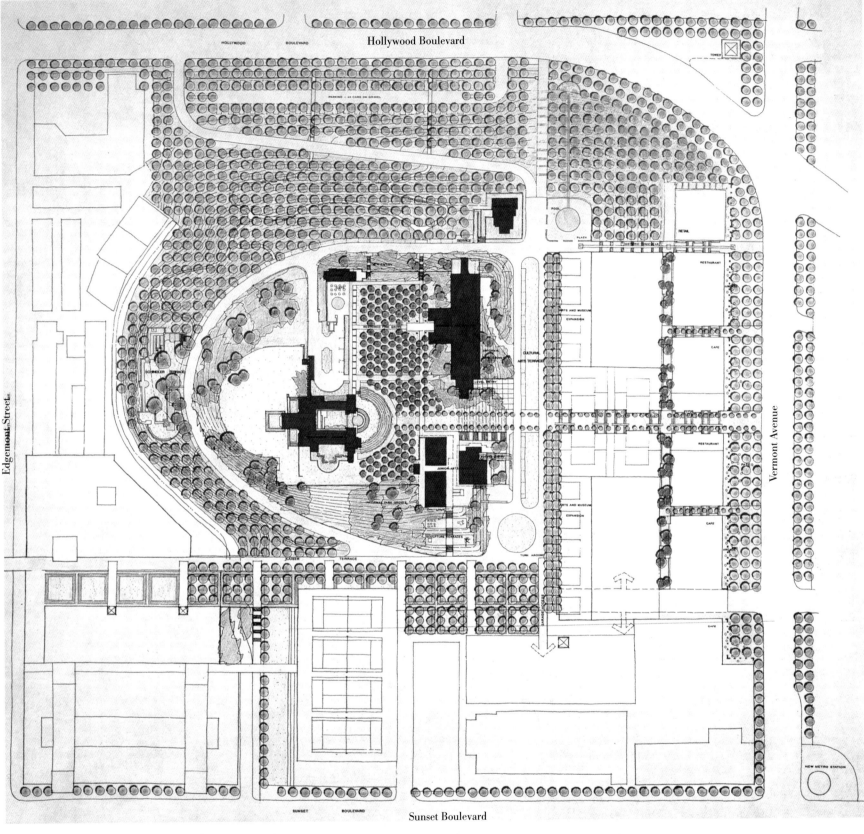

Hollywood Boulevard

Sunset Boulevard

Edgemont Street

Vermont Avenue

1995 Barnsdall Park Master Plan: 1,763 trees proposed

0   200 feet

ART CENTER COLLEGE OF DESIGN

Schindler's Terrace, with its pergola, fountains and wading pool; and the seven gardens immediately surrounding Hollyhock House, which were originally planted according to Barnsdall's preferences for gradations of color. These gardens should be restored to their original scale and texture, bearing in mind the realities of present day maintenance and costs.

A range of functional considerations are addressed in Phase I, including pedestrian and vehicular circulation, handicapped access, parking, security fencing, lighting and signage. The potential for relocating some of the arts programs that have outgrown their present facilities is addressed more specifically in the second phase of planning.

Phase II considers the ways in which a restored and revitalized Barnsdall Park will inevitably improve the city. An idealistic, hopeful vision, it attempts to revive much of the dream that brought Aline Barnsdall to Southern California: the flourishing of artistic and cultural expression in a setting of exceptional natural beauty. This phase of the master plan also assumes a measure of freedom that Barnsdall herself always wanted to enjoy on her own terms. It does not imitate previous architectural schemes or the particular siting of a facility, for instance, but it does accommodate some things, such as a theatre, which Barnsdall did not, in the end, have built. It introduces a tower, a feature that Wright would have erected in the late 1950s; but this tower does not resemble Wright's at all! The new tower is taller, more angular, and entirely of its own time, the 1990s. It is sited where it can announce the presence of Barnsdall Park in the city. In effect, the tower helps to extend the park, in order that it may embrace and enhance the city that has developed around it.

In turn, the planners hope that the city will begin to follow the lead of the Park, particularly regarding four areas: Street Edges, the Corner Precinct, the Terraces and the Hilltop.

To date, there is no coherent economic vision for the district surrounding Barnsdall Park, just as there is little functional interaction among the several neighbors. Unplanned development has led to a series of negative impacts which this phase of the master plan must address, notably, the blocked ground-level views up to the park, the "back door" conditions along the park's edges; the lack of pedestrian scale along the streets; and the loss of Olive Hill as either natural slope or built form. To improve these conditions, a public/private partnership could be formed for the mutual benefit of the park and its neighbors—perhaps following the successful model of the recent Bryant Park restoration in New York City.

At Barnsdall Park, the urban revitalization could begin with a generous infusion of one historic element: trees. The master plan recommends the extension of the olive grove to both sides of Vermont Avenue and Hollywood Boulevard. A 30-foot wide tree-lined promenade, or Paseo, could also be provided along Vermont Avenue between Hollywood and Sunset Boulevards. Here, some people would enjoy a leisurely stroll beneath the olives that will be trimmed up to create a pleasant canopy. Others, bent on one of many destinations for business or pleasure, will surely pass more quickly; and they, too, will be accommodated in this paseo, a major pedestrian link between the future Metro station, the park, and its commercial and institutional neighbors.

Reflecting Wright's unbuilt scheme, of 1920, for a line of shops along Hollywood Boulevard, any new development of the shopping center along Vermont Avenue should face both outward and inward: continuous retail shops facing the street, for instance, and arts-related uses facing the park. Paths, stairways, and terraces could all provide better pedestrian access to the park. And people using Metro Rail and other forms of public transportation could be informed of the opportunities for linking trips to Barnsdall Park, Griffith Park and Observatory, the Greek Theater, and other destinations.

At the northeast corner—the original entrance to Olive Hill—the olive orchard could be re-established on land that faces the new "North Corner Park." With some street closing and re-routing of traffic, this new entrance, marked by a tower, could reconnect the park to the streets that once gave definition to Olive Hill. On higher ground, the terraces could offer a range of activities, from passive recreation to cultural activities and festivals. The extension and rebuilding of one terrace could encourage a sharing of amenities between the hospital and the park: not only the parking garage, but also spaces for passive recreation, gardens for healing, and views of fine landscape for those confined indoors.

From the vantage point of the Hilltop, the reopening of splendid distant views over the Los Angeles basin, the mountains, and the ocean is one priority that respects the donor's original intentions. The master plan recommends that any future expansion of buildings within or near the park should entail a carefully considered massing that steps down the hillside. It encourages roof gardens, terraces, and other means of visually extending and complementing the park. And, in one bold stroke, it proposes a major stairway, an amenity that could be created by "slicing" through the existing commercial structures on Vermont Avenue. This fine east/west vista could be enjoyed on many levels, most dramatically from the hilltop grove of pines and eucalyptus, east of Hollyhock House.

In the end, who will benefit? Who will come to the restored and revitalized Barnsdall Park? The presence of a major work by Frank Lloyd Wright will always be an attraction to visitors from other parts of the city, the nation, and the world. Along with the four other houses in the Los Angeles region that Wright designed in the 1920s (the nearby Ennis, Storer, and Freeman houses, and the Millard House, in Pasadena), Hollyhock House and its grounds will remain a destination for anyone who is curious to experience, at first hand, something of Wright's feeling for the integration of land and buildings.

There are also many other people in East Hollywood whose curiosity has yet to be piqued by the work of Wright and the vision of Barnsdall. Some speak Spanish as a first language, some Japanese, some Vietnamese, some Chinese, some Armenian. To the south of Barnsdall Park, the mother tongue is likely to be Spanish or Asian; there, for less than half the population, it is English. In the hills to the north and east, families tend to be smaller and incomes are higher. On the flatlands closer to the park, families tend to have lower incomes and more children. In the planning for Barnsdall Park, this diverse population and their interests, needs, and imaginations have been considered. The glimpses of the park from street level, the experiences on terraces and hilltop, and the views outward should be theirs, as well. In time, perhaps some of them will be moved to mine for beauty as well as for gold.

The Vision

Just as Frank Lloyd Wright had to revise his master plan for Barnsdall Park again and again to respond first to Aline Barnsdall's dynamism and then to the dynamic changes occurring in Southern California, the designers of the new master plan have had to address a series of new situations that had not been addressed in the earlier plans by Wright. In 1995, a simple re-creation or completion of any of the historic plans was not possible.

Certain qualities and features could be restored: the mood and ambience of Hollyhock House and its grounds, the shape and style of the land form, and the original plantings on the hilltop. The visual presence of Olive Hill itself had been greatly reduced, however, and its relation to the neighborhood and the district had been irrevocably altered by the institutional and commercial uses at the base of the hill and by the surrounding urban growth.

The new master plan therefore sets out to both repair and re-create as well as to initiate. It calls for the repair and replanting of the hilltop and environs to restore the condition described in the earlier master plans and landscape plans by Wright and his son Lloyd Wright. It proposes to regrade the hillsides to softer contours and to realign the roads to more gentle grades, conducive to leisurely walking and driving—experiences that stir memories of the 1920s. The plan also proposes to revise the parking to fit within the park landscape rather than allow cars to dominate the land use.

The master plan proposes to narrow, but also to define and secure, the great axial views created by Wright. The historic olive grove is to be replanted in a new dynamic form. The defining element of the grove—its agricultural character—will thus reach out into the neighborhood as a visual symbol of the rightful importance and place of Barnsdall Park.

To connect the new Metro Station back to the park, the master plan proposes a new commercial "paseo" of shops and cafes, a place that people will perceive as lively, sociable, and non-threatening. The paseo would further unify the proposed new commercial development with the entry to Kaiser Hospital and with the proposed new commercial space at the new corner entry to the park. According to the plan, the olive grove will be extended and, honoring Wright's earlier vision, a redesigned water feature will be sited on the corner.

Finally, along with the rebuilding of the historic Schindler Terrace, the master plan calls for the creation of two new terraces to connect the rear of the proposed new commercial center with the Arts Center and the Museum. Also, the rear of the Kaiser complex is to be connected with the park. In the process, the existing "back doors" will become front doors.

By these acts of design, the master plan proposes to transform the great legacy of Aline Barnsdall and Frank Lloyd Wright into a living and dynamic center within the cultural life of modern Los Angeles.

Model of the 1995 Master Plan

Barnsdall Park 1995: Existing Site Conditions

Topography

Topography remains the single most dominant characteristic of Barnsdall Park. Although the visual quality of Olive Hill has been increasingly degraded by multi-story commercial and institutional buildings, the hill itself is recognizable from all over the surrounding region. Hilltop spaces provide separation and a sense of refuge from the city below. Abrupt grade changes, created by the existing access road and off-site retaining walls, disrupt the once gently-sloping transition from the flat urban landscape to the hilltop above.

The topography alone affects many functions on the site. Steep grades require stairways to accommodate pedestrian circulation; in turn, these stairways prevent the handicapped from freely entering some facilities. On the hilltop, the limited space is a major constraint to the expansion of built facilities. On the steep slopes, any additional buildings would be costly to construct. More feasible would be the leveling of slopes for outdoor spaces, to be used for gatherings, passive recreation, and the display of artwork.

Circulation

Internal site circulation includes roads, ramps, stairs, and paved walkways that respond to each facility's requirements but do not contribute to a unified whole. No system of circulation links buildings to one another and to the various site facilities. In some cases, curbs, walls, and stairs form barriers to disabled persons seeking access to site facilities.

Pedestrian access from Vermont Avenue and the corner of Vermont and Hollywood is deficient. Retaining walls built when the edges of the site were developed create insurmountable barriers along three of the four edges of the site. The forthcoming Metro station will probably increase the flow of pedestrians from Vermont Avenue to the site.

Views

Views relate directly to topography and edge development. Unobstructed panoramic views from the hilltop have been constricted to narrow view corridors between off-site buildings. Distant views of Barnsdall Park are blocked by neighboring buildings that are destined for future growth.

Many park spaces look down on the unsightly service access areas of surrounding developments. Views of Olive Hill are cut off by these developments, such that the Hill has no visual connection to the surrounding city. Trees remaining from the original planting continue to be the primary vertical element that identifies the park from afar.

Historic Structures

The structures designed by Frank Lloyd Wright were conceived with inseparable bonds to the site; they complement the topographical form and frame distant views of the city below. Currently, Hollyhock House, its Garage, the Pergola, the Spring House, and Residence A most clearly recall the architectural dynamism and elegance of Wright's work. Schindler's Terrace, although historically and architecturally significant, lies in ruins.

These structures, in various states of disrepair, form the central historical elements of the park. They also provide a variety of programmatic uses. The spatial resources are overtaxed, however, particularly at Residence A, which houses the Barnsdall Arts Center (BAC). Overall, the site can scarcely absorb any expansion of programs for the cultural arts.

Other Structures

The Municipal Art Gallery (MAG) and Junior Arts Center (JAC) are necessary interventions on Olive Hill. As community resources that support important cultural activities, they are invaluable in fulfilling Barnsdall Park's mandate as an arts park. As substantial additions to the original site plan by Frank Lloyd Wright, however, these buildings tend to clutter the hilltop, limit views, and produce an unintended campus-like network of paths and ramps on the hilltop ground plane. Attempts at architectural cohesion have been minimally successful. As a result, from many perspectives, Hollyhock House no longer appears to be the preeminent architectural element on the site.

Roads and Paths

Over the years, roads in the park have changed significantly in both their appearance and their location. Overall, the original sense of the rural landscape has been lost through modern road construction. The addition of curbs and gutters has visually transformed the once rural character of park roads to suburban standards.

Perpendicular parking has been added haphazardly along roads, cutting or filling the slopes with little sensitivity to the original topography or rural character of Olive Hill. Hilltop parking occurs throughout the site, imposing the automobile on many landscape spaces. For events held in the park, overflow parking is accommodated at the off-site facilities of the Kaiser Permanente garage; however, there is as yet no pedestrian connection between this facility and the Hilltop.

There is currently no cohesive network of paths throughout the site. Internal circulation follows a maze of concrete ramps and railings, walkways, and stairs, with minimal sense of hierarchy, sequence, progression, and entry. There is no handicapped accessibility between street level and the Hilltop.

Landscape Character

Before improvements by Frank Lloyd Wright and Aline Barnsdall, Olive Hill's landscape was defined by the agricultural grid of olive trees. This 18- to 20-foot grid formed the primary module for Wright's site plan and the layout of Hollyhock House. The olive trees remained a significant component of Wright's vision for Olive Hill. The landscape design for Olive Hill, executed by Wright's son Lloyd Wright, consisted of three concentric zones, each becoming less formal as it radiated out from Hollyhock House.

The Hilltop zone surrounding Hollyhock House was comprised of planting beds, manicured lawns, and water gardens extending the formal spaces of the house into a series of outdoor rooms. These garden spaces formed a sharp contrast to the geometric pine and olive groves, allowing one to emerge from the agricultural landscape onto a garden plinth upon which the house rested. The next lower zone, made up of drought-tolerant species of Oleander, acacia, jacaranda, and so forth, extended to the grove road. The third zone was the olive grove itself. This zone received very little treatment other than the addition of groundcovers and the replacement of lost trees.

Although very degraded in appearance today, these zones still reflect a sense of Wright's original intent. Worn and neglected garden and courtyard spaces continue to provide a sense of contrast to the Pine and Olive groves. The remaining Pine and Eucalyptus trees ultimately provide the singular statement of Olive Hill's topographical form as they tower over the buildings along the edges. Finally, the remaining Olive trees, now down to less than 10% of their original number, still convey a sense of the site's agricultural history and Wright's original site planning and landscape design.

The simplicity and elegance of Wright's original design provides flexible outdoor spaces that are adaptable for many uses. As some of these spaces deteriorated, however, people have tended to avoid them. In time, such spaces appear unsafe, especially at night. Once restored, these spaces should invite a variety of uses—particularly in the favorable climate of Los Angeles, which supports outdoor uses nearly year-round.

Barnsdall Park looking east, 1989.

The 1995 Master Plan: Recommendations

The Landscape

Hilltop Gardens

The gardens and lawns surrounding the house were originally designed with a progression from geometric pine groves at the hilltop to manicured beds and lawns around the house and outbuildings. Encouraged by Aline Barnsdall, Lloyd Wright was acutely attentive to details of the landscape. Now these fine details, along with the overall geometry and character of the various theme gardens, have been lost. Important views from the crown of the hill and Hollyhock House have been blocked by trees.

The master plan recommends that the character and purpose of these lawns and gardens be re-established. They provide the opportunity for unique and varied settings for performances, festivals, and classes, and restored views to Downtown Hollywood, Century City, Marina Del Rey, and the Pacific Ocean.

The Pine Grove

The Wrights designed this grove of Stone Pines and Eucalyptus trees to counterbalance the mass and color of Hollyhock House. Viewed from outside the park, this mature grove extends the verticality of the hill, enhancing the contrast between level plane and hill. The master plan proposes that this grove be replanted with a wider spacing of trees to allow more light to filter through the trees to the ground plane, which can then be used for art classes, smaller gatherings, and festivals.

Critical long range views can be channeled through the evergreen trees. The primary entries to the adjacent institutions should be re-oriented to the new Arts Terrace below, restoring the more domestic scale of the Hollyhock gardens at the hilltop.

Hollyhock House Motor Court

The master plan recommends that the original parterres of lawn and paving be restored to re-establish the original scale of the space and entry sequence to the house. The primary access to the house, from the Motor Court and along the Pet Pergola, can be enhanced with the addition of a bookstore/cafe with moveable tables and umbrellas.

Pine Grove

Hollyhock House lawn

Plan view of renewed great lawn and pool (model)

View toward renewed entry with garage/bookstore and cafe (model)

Replanted pine grove (model)

Hollyhock House gardens (model)

New entry drive (model)

View of restored pine grove

Hilltop Perimeter

This zone frames the crown of the hill and provides a transition between the gridded olive grove and the more domestic planting palette of the pine groves and the gardens near the house. The master plan recommends a considerable amount of new planting. Vegetation will frame the fine remaining views of Los Angeles and soften the reconstructed loop road and associated parking without disturbing long range views, while screening undesirable views of adjacent buildings, service areas, and parking lots.

Olive Groves

Of the original 1,154 trees planted by a previous owner in 1890, fewer than 10% remain today. The image and the presence of the grove was so strong that Wright based his master plan for the entire site on the 20-foot tree grid. This great agricultural grove extended from the edge of the crown to the base of the slope in all directions.

The master plan re-establishes the historic gridded Olive Grove in order to restore the powerful visual image the park once possessed. The grove's agricultural qualities will evoke the historic purpose of the land, and the presence of the grove will boldly reconnect the park to the city.

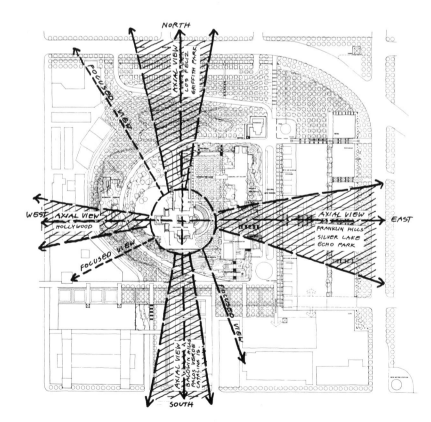

Proposed improvements: view diagram

Existing view toward Hollywood Hills

Hollyhock House seen over Schindler Terrace (model)

View toward South Terrace and Kaiser Hospital (model)

Corner view to Residence A (model)

View of Hollyhock House from preserved view corridor at West Lawn

Preservation of Historic Site Planning and the Hollyhock Axis

The historic legacy of the park is outstanding. In addition to Hollyhock House and Residence A, the hilltop acropolis with its terraces, sight lines, groves, and gardens, all designed by Frank Lloyd Wright, are worthy of historic recognition and preservation. This is the only property designed by Wright and his son Lloyd Wright that is currently used as a city-owned public park. Moreover, this is possibly the most complete example of Wright's talents in the design of the land.

The Hollyhock axis could recreate one of Wright's most important gestures, beginning at Hollyhock House and proceeding through the gardens, the park, and the new Arts Terrace, through the rebuilt shopping center, and to the neighborhoods beyond. It would provide identification, orientation, spectacular framed views, and access artistically worthy of Wright's historic contribution.

The New Terraces

Overview

The adjacent developments have yielded under-used spaces, treated as backyards, on three of the park edges. These edges are functionally and physically disconnected from the Hilltop, blocking visual and physical access to the park from the streets.

Opportunities for shared facilities between the park and its neighbors lie in sloped areas in the park that are currently under-used and nearly inaccessible. The master plan recommends that new terraces be built in these areas, so as to increase the amount of useable space for passive recreation, artistic and cultural activities, and festivals. The master plan also envisions that the creation of these terraces will encourage the development of new "front door" relationships between the park and the adjacent uses on three edges of the park.

The Arts Terrace

The creation of a mid-level terrace can recapture blighted areas of the park and transform them into spaces for both active and passive recreation. The Arts Terrace will become the entrance to the park as well as the center of the park's family of institutions. It will allow for a much greater variety of passive recreation and art-related activities.

The sensitive grading, road construction, and planting recommended by the master plan will improve areas for dropping off pedestrians and recapture spaces for campus recreation. On the east side of this terrace, the upper portion of the rebuilt shopping center can provide expanded offices and studios for the museum and arts centers, a new theater, and cafes and restaurants, to serve both the neighborhood and the revived park.

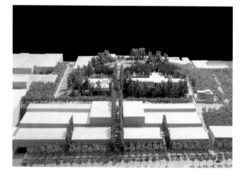

Axial connection from Vermont Street (model)

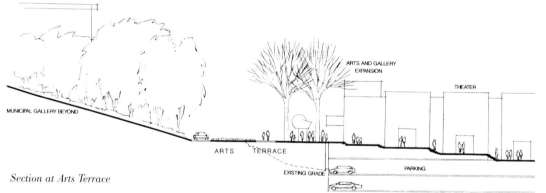

Section at Arts Terrace

Regraded Arts Terrace, Phase I (model)

View of proposed Arts Terrace looking north from Hollyhock House axis with museum at left, museum shops and offices at right

The Arts Terrace can connect Residence A to the arts-related buildings (JAC, MAG, BAC, etc.) and to the Kaiser parking structure. The master plan recommends new lighting and security to ensure the safety of pedestrians. A pedestrian and vehicular bridge connecting the Terrace and the existing Kaiser parking structure will provide for staff and visitor parking at Barnsdall Park.

The South Terrace

The South Terrace is seen as an outdoor garden and recreation area for the staff and patients at the hospital as well as for park visitors. The master plan envisions several potential uses here: a formal parterre, areas for active and passive recreation, and perhaps a cafe or cafeteria outlet.

Schindler's Terrace

The Schindler Terrace, perhaps the most degraded built element in the park, was originally intended as a place for children. As an important historic element of the park, this terrace should be completely restored, with its fountains, sunny and shady sitting areas, wading pools, and hanging gardens.

New Arts Terrace (model)

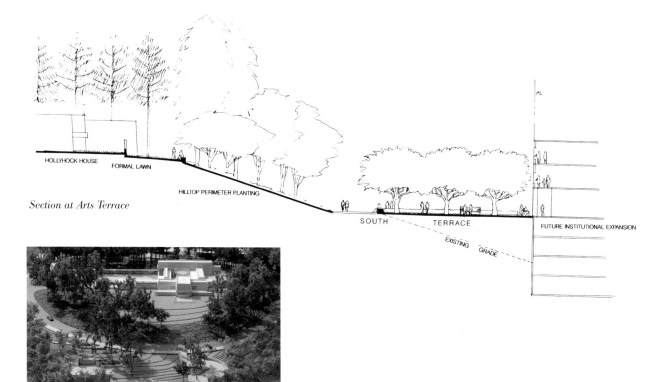

Section at Arts Terrace

Rebuilt Schindler's Terrace (model)

View of proposed Arts Terrace at Junior Arts Center and Museum, looking north from bridge at Kaiser garage

Circulation and Movement

Roads, Paths, and Parking

The natural topography has been altered by roads and parking designed to suburban standards. The curbs, gutters, and retaining walls to accommodate them have disrupted the natural topography.

The master plan proposes that all roads and parking areas be rebuilt to fit into the revised topography. Existing retaining walls and curbs should be removed, and parking lots should assume the rural character of orchards. Parking should be eliminated from all historically significant open spaces. Overflow parking can be accommodated by parallel parking along the shoulders of roads, a common practice in the 1920s.

The master plan includes a winding handicapped-accessible path system, below 5% grade, throughout the groves, from the street level to the hilltop, serving all institutions within the Park.

Agreements should be made with adjacent landowners to provide overflow and event parking, along with improved pedestrian access to the park.

Street Edges

Commercial, institutional, and residential development, as well as the Metro Rail construction on Hollywood Boulevard, have caused the park to lose possession of, and connection to, the edges of the streets. In the process, the park has also lost its identity, viewed from the streets below. Furthermore, both the park institutions and the commercial and institutional developments lack a coherent economic vision at the district level.

The completion of the Metro Rail station and system will connect the Park to a new regional transportation infrastructure. Today, however, the new MTA station is disconnected from both Barnsdall Park and Los Feliz Village to the north. The hospitals and their large populations are also disconnected from the park and Los Feliz Village. The streets surrounding the Park lack pedestrian scale and identity.

The master plan recommends that the Olive grove be extended to both sides of Hollywood Boulevard and Vermont Avenue as street trees, using the 20-foot grid spacing of the grove. This new planting will create a distinctive streetscape vocabulary around the Olive Hill block, and mark the intersection of each pedestrian/vehicular connection to the Hilltop with clarity and distinction. Property owners, political entities, and community groups will be encouraged to utilize common resources and to form economic partnerships to benefit the park and the district, for their mutual advantage.

The master plan proposes an elegant, 30-foot wide, specially paved promenade lined with olive trees in order to create an arcaded Paseo, together with ground floor retail, along Vermont Avenue between Sunset and Hollywood, and on Hollywood Boulevard, between Vermont and Edgemont. Commercial interests and institutions should take full advantage of opportunities to add axial pedestrian corridors into the park. The Hollyhock axis provides the opportunity to develop a route from Vermont Avenue, through the adjacent commercial property. New points of access benefit both the park and the neighborhood. Similar connections should be considered through Hollywood Boulevard and Edgemont and Sunset (through Kaiser Hospital). New development should face the street with continuous retail, and should also face the park with uses related to the arts and cultural activity.

Existing road with concrete curb

Existing grade with stairs

View to north of proposed Paseo on Vermont Avenue with shops and cafes (model)

View to south on Vermont Avenue (model)

Recommended multi-level buildings along Vermont Avenue edge (model)

North slope grove seen along Olive Hill Road

Corner and North Corner Park

Existing commercial development on the corner of Vermont Avenue, Prospect Street and Hollywood Boulevard has eliminated the historic corner entry to the park, and has reinforced the park's isolation from the city. It has also greatly altered the pedestrian scale of the neighborhood and blocked important views of Residence A.

The master plan proposes to extend the park around the corner, recreating a powerful, memorable park presence at this important gateway, and extending the Olive Grove planting concepts into the corner precinct during interim and future redevelopment. Recognizing the corner's commercial value, as well, the master plan advocates the concept of *shared space*—Retail in the Park. The plan envisions a dynamic, active new park space in the city that will connect the corner with the park by means of an escalator or other mechanical staircase.

A new North Corner Park could be created by closing Prospect Avenue between Vermont and Hollywood Boulevard, and connecting the existing triangle to the city at its north. A new Barnsdall Tower in the North Corner Park would bring Barnsdall Park to the street level at this critical corner. The tower would also serve as a monumental starting point and terminus to Hollywood Boulevard and the Los Feliz Village retail corridor. As monument and signage, it would announce this place as a major gateway to Barnsdall Park, Griffith Park, and Hollywood. It would be seen as one approaches from downtown, from Highway 101, from Griffith Park, and from Hollywood.

Olive trees on both sides of Vermont Avenue looking towards tower (model)

Proposed North Corner Park and Stair at Hollywood Boulevard and Vermont Avenue (model)

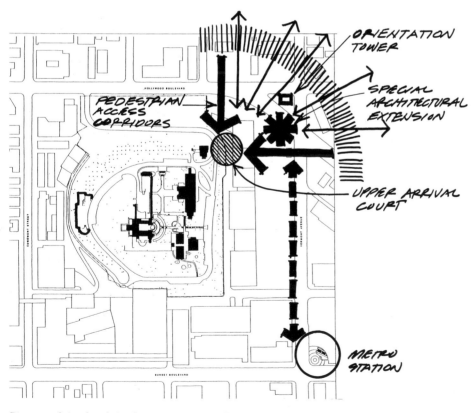

Diagram of visual and circulation extensions in the vicinity of North Corner Park

Hollywood Boulevard east to North Corner Park and Tower (model)

Proposed orientation tower at Hollywood Boulevard and Vermont Avenue (model)

The Sections

Multi-level buildings can maximize the use of lower levels for parking and service behind the street. Vertical circulation could connect the street-side commercial buildings to upper park levels. Stepped development on adjacent properties should respect the park and relate to the terraces. Upper-level commercial development should have park-related programs.

Commercial activity would enliven the Terraces and bring greater safety to these levels of the park. Cooperative development on adjacent properties would result in further improvements for both the park and the neighboring properties.

The master plan proposes to re-open and preserve view corridors from the Hilltop outward: to the south, to Los Angeles and Catalina, to Marina del Rey, Century City, the Pacific Ocean, and the Santa Monica Mountains; to the west, to the heart of Hollywood; to the northwest, to the Hollywood sign and the AFI; to the north, to Griffith Observatory, Frank Lloyd Wright's Ennis House and Richard Neutra's Lovell House, the Los Feliz Hills and Griffith Park, and views of the San Gabriel Mountains and Franklin Hill.

Grading

Regrading and reshaping the entire site will serve both functional and cultural purposes. The gentler grades will increase accessibility for the handicapped and offer a sense of continuity that will help to orient all visitors. Moreover, as the land is restored to its original, historic character, the park will regain the sense of wholeness that has been lost over the years of careless development, both immediately outside and also inside the park.

The master plan outlines specific measures to be taken: the hillsides will be carefully reshaped; the roads, terraces, gardens, and parking will all be coordinated; and the amount of recently-built utilitarian steps, rails, and concrete walls will be reduced to a minimum. In the end, these efforts to restore a sense of history will enhance possibilities for the present and the future, as well. There will emerge a dignified, elegant base for a complete replanting of the park and for a wider range of recreational arts activities within the park.

View from Olive Hill

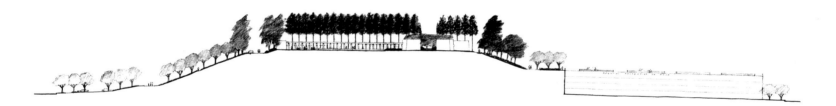

Proposed site cross section North/South

Proposed site cross section East/West

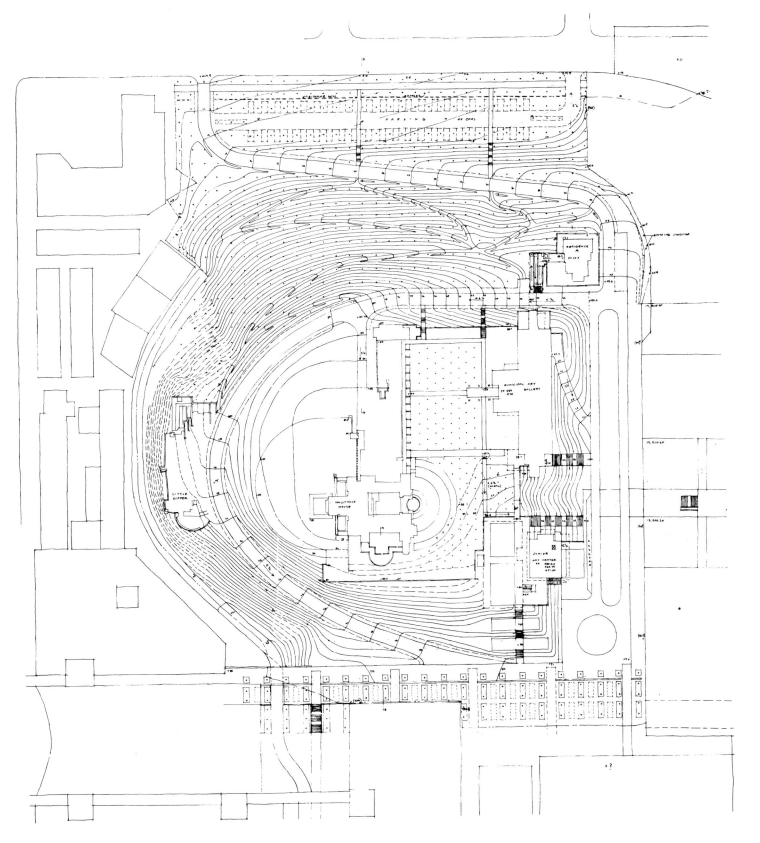

Proposed regrading plan

Phasing

The renovation of Barnsdall Park is proposed in four phases.

Phase 1.a

Rebuilds the large open slope toward Hollywood Boulevard, providing a new walkable entrance for the park, new street-level parking and the first large replanting of the olive groves.

Phase 1.b

Restores the historic gardens and lawns around Hollyhock House, replants the pine grove and hilltop periphery, and builds the first half of the new Arts Terrace and Residence A Plaza.

Phase 2.a

In conjunction with the rebuilding of the shopping center, this phase produces the new corner pedestrian entrance, the Paseo linking the Metro Station with the sidewalk commercial buildings, the corner, and, through the rebuilt Hollyhock axis, a new pedestrian entry upwards into the park. This phase also completes the Arts Terrace with shops, arts office and studio space, and the new theater, and adds shared parking beneath the shopping center.

Phase 2.b

In conjunction with the future development of the Kaiser Hospital, this phase produces the joint South Terrace, which connects the upper Hospital floors directly with the park at a pedestrian level, and institutionalizes the southern view corridor to the Pacific Ocean.

Phase I model

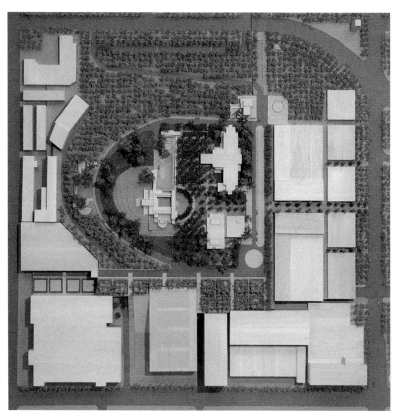

Phase II model

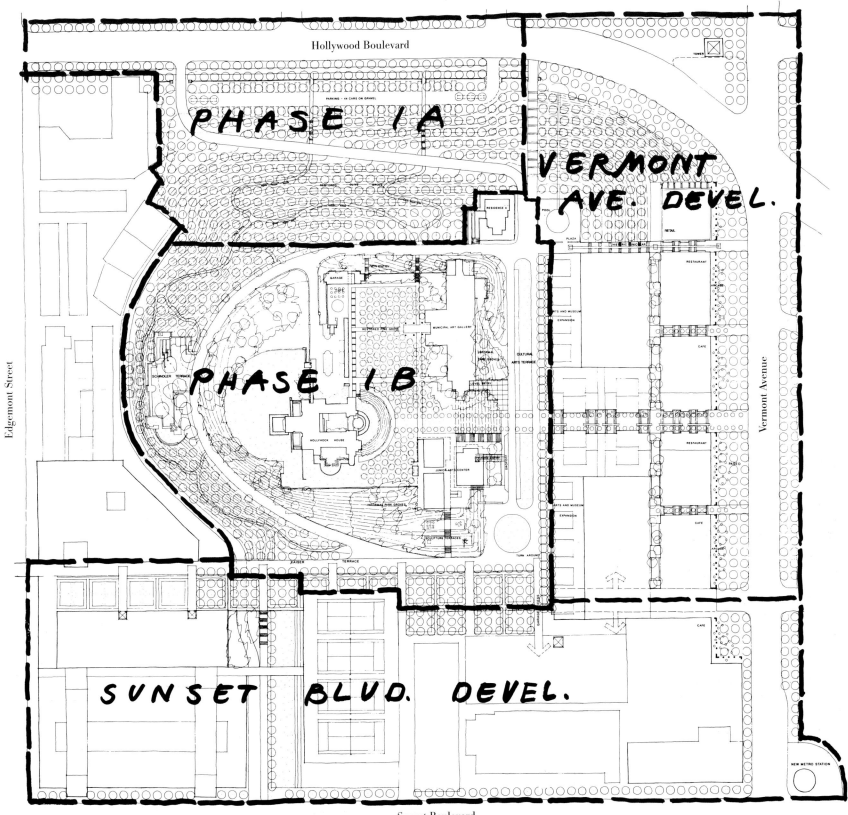

PHASE IA

VERMONT AVE. DEVEL.

PHASE IB

SUNSET BLVD. DEVEL.

Hollywood Boulevard

Edgemont Street

Vermont Avenue

Sunset Boulevard

Phasing plan

0   200 feet

Appendix

Notes

Credits

Appendix

General Principles

In November 1991, the Barnsdall Park Board of Overseer's Planning and Development Committee issued a statement of General Principles outlining the following strategy for the revitalization of Olive Hill:

1. The Barnsdall Art Park is an art Park — its future should remain centered on advancement and enjoyment of the arts. Organized art-oriented events may reflect the many cultures of Los Angeles. Passive recreation opportunities should allow visitors to take advantage of the Park as significant open space in the City.

2. Olive Hill, its topography, and its open space, are the essence of this site in the urban landscape. All future actions should restore and reinforce these characteristics.

3. An historical site report and a master plan must be prepared to inform future decisions about Park restoration and development. The site itself is historically significant and includes elements of great historic and cultural value. Any projects that may need to go forward prior to the completion of the historic site survey should be planned with regard to these general principles as well as the extensive historic materials that are readily available for reference.

4. The Park must become more visually and physically accessible: views of the Park and its significant features from major vantage points in the area should be preserved and enhanced; entrances should be strongly developed for vehicular and pedestrian access from Barnsdall Avenue, in relation to the historic Hollywood Boulevard/Vermont Avenue intersection, and a revised Hollywood Boulevard entrance; roads and parking within the site should serve normal daily activities; peak parking requirements should be accommodated through arrangements with adjacent landowners.

5. New design and construction should reverse the existing "backside" character of the Park's relationship to adjacent properties. Significant rehabilitation and enhancement of the periphery should include site development and projects that complement the general principles of this strategic plan and improve the integration of the Park and its environs. New projects on adjacent sites should be required to positively attend to the Park and to respect primary view corridors. Similarly, any planning for the Park should proceed with due regard to adjacent development.

6. The function of the Barnsdall Art Park Board of Overseers as a planning consortium must be fully realized. The board includes commissioners and general managers of primary City Departments as well as residential neighbors and principal institutional and commercial entities. Full participation at the highest levels by all parties is required to coordinate the future development of the Park and its environs. The Planning and Development Committee should serve the Board of Overseers to review all current and future planning proposals and designs in relation to this strategic Plan and to initiate suggestions for the Park.

Mission Statement

The intent of the Master Plan is to develop and provide tools to set forth a clear vision and achievable goals for Barnsdall Park. This vision will be based on the significant architectural and cultural resources in place, and the dynamics of the Park's constituency. The Master Plan Team utilized multi-disciplinary expertise to address key elements of the site's historic past, existing rich and diverse cultural life, and the future use which will be affected by adjacent development and increase with the regional access provided by Metro Rail.

Critical areas of the Master Plan Study included:
Garnering and responding to the community's concerns, local opinions and values, involvement of the Park administrators, planning consortium, arts community, residential, commercial, and institutional stakeholders.

Examination and analysis of the physical site, opportunities and constraints afforded by this island within the City. Issues of accessibility and safety were studied.

Weighing of preservation and conservation issues related to the historic significance of this internationally recognized resource.

Analysis of transportation and circulation systems within and around the Park.

Translation of visionary planning concepts into high-caliber design proposals for the Park's physical renovation as well as the adjacent land use affecting the Park itself.

Development of a powerful and positive image for the Park, restoring its reputation in the community.

Research of potential funding and implementation strategies involving City, State, Federal, not-for-profit, public/private partnership, and on-site income generation possibilities.

Notes

Introduction

1. Donald Hoffmann, *Frank Lloyd Wright's Hollyhock House* (New York: Dover, 1992), 102-103. See also "The Client," Note 1.

2. See Anthony Alofsin, *Frank Lloyd Wright – The Lost Years, 1910-1922: A Study of Influence* (Chicago: University of Chicago Press, 1993).

3. Reyner Banham, "The Wilderness Years of Frank Lloyd Wright," *Journal of the Royal Institute of British Architects* (December, 1969), 512-519.

The Land

1. Raymond F. Dasmann, *The Destruction of California* (New York: Macmillan, 1965), 16.

2. Anthony Alofsin, *Frank Lloyd Wright – The Lost Years*, 288. See also Bruce A. Bolt, *Earthquakes* (New York: W.H. Freeman, 1988), 63, 185.

3. John McPhee, *Assembling California* (New York: Farrar, Straus and Giroux, 1993), 9, 47, 180.

4. Michael L. Smith, *Pacific Visions: California Scientists and the Environment: 1850-1915* (New Haven: Yale University Press, 1987), 28-53.

5. Ibid.

6. James D. Houston, *Californians: Searching for the Golden State* (Berkeley: Donald S. Ellis/Creative Arts Book Co., 1985), 18; Dasmann, *Destruction of California*, 23-24; and Kevin Starr, *Inventing the Dream: California Through the Progressive Era* (New York: Oxford University Press, 1985), 8-11.

7. McPhee, *Assembling California*, 5, 107-9, 182.

8. Ibid., 276-78.

9. Victoria Padilla, *Southern California Gardens: An Illustrated History* (Berkeley: University of California Press, 1961), 3-29. See also *Barnsdall Park Historic Site Survey*, in "The Client," Note 1.

10. Charles Dudley Warner, *Our Italy* (New York: Harper & Bros., 1891), 18, 40-41.

11. Padilla, *Southern California Gardens*, 12-98.

12. *Sunset Western Garden Book*, 4th ed. (Menlo Park, Calif.: Lane Publishing Co., 1986), 8-29.

13. Carey McWilliams, "The Discovery of Los Angeles" (1978), in *Unknown California*, ed. Jonathan Eisen and David Fine (New York: Macmillan, 1985), 188-89.

The Client

1. Biographical information for this chapter is derived mainly from Kathryn Smith, "Frank Lloyd Wright, Hollyhock House, and Olive Hill, 1914-1924," *Journal of the Society of Architectural Historians* (March, 1979), 15-33; Smith, *Frank Lloyd Wright, Hollyhock House and Olive Hill: Buildings and Projects for Aline Barnsdall* (New York: Rizzoli, 1992); Barnsdall Park Historic Site Survey (June, 1995), prepared for the City of Los Angeles by Levin & Associates, with contributions by Kathryn Smith; and Donald Hoffmann, *Frank Lloyd Wright's Hollyhock House* (New York: Dover, 1992).

2. George Bernard Shaw, "The Womanly Woman," from *The Quintessence of Ibsenism* (1891), in Shaw, *Selected Plays and Other Writings* (New York: Holt, Reinhart and Winston, 1956), 44-50.

3. Lawrence Langner, *The Magic Curtain* (New York: E.P. Dutton, 1951), 58-64. Donald Hoffmann identified the real "Celeste" in his *Hollyhock House*, 6-7. Langner was a patent attorney who later turned playwright and founded the Theatre Guild in New York City.

4. Constance D'Arcy Mackay, *The Little Theatre in the United States* (New York: Henry Holt & Co., 1917), 10-12.

5. Norman Bel Geddes, *Miracle in the Evening* (Garden City, New York: Doubleday, 1960), 173. According to Geddes, Barnsdall's studies with Duse would have taken place about 1910-1911.

6. Edward Gordon Craig, *On the Art of the Theatre* (Boston: Small, Maynard & Co., 1924); see especially Craig's "The Artists of the Theatre of the Future" (1907), reprinted here.

7. Reproductions of Craig's sets appear in Craig, *Art of the Theatre*, and in James W. Flannery, *W.B. Yeats and the Idea of a Theatre: The Early Abbey Theatre in Theory and Practice* (Toronto: Macmillan, 1976).

8. Mary Caroline Crawford, *The Romance of the American Theatre* (Boston: Little, Brown, and Co., 1925), 490.

9. Yeats to Miss Florence Darragh (March 28, 1913), quoted in Flannery, *Yeats and the Idea of a Theatre*, 276.

10. A description, photograph and plan of the Arena Goldoni appear in Sheldon Cheney, *The Open-Air Theatre* (New York: Mitchell Kennerley, 1918), 43-46.

11. Esther McCoy, *Vienna to Los Angeles: Two Journeys* (Santa Monica, Calif.: Arts + Architecture Press, 1979), 79.

12. Aline Barnsdall to Norman Bel Geddes (November 30, 1915), quoted in Smith, *Frank Lloyd Wright* (1992), 18.

13. See Aline Barnsdall to Frank Lloyd Wright (February 4, 1926), in Bruce Brooks Pfeiffer, ed., *Letters to Clients: Frank Lloyd Wright* (Fresno: The Press at California State University, 1986), 38-39. Barnsdall wrote, "You will never know me if you don't come to realize that I have never known fear in that or any other moral sense, that I am only at home and interested on unchartered [sic] seas."

14. Mackay, *Little Theatre in the United States*, 14-15.

15. Ibid., 156-158. Mackay writes that Barnsdall's production of *Alice in Wonderland*, most successfully given in New York, was memorable for its unerring casting and its delightful, whimsical scenery. See also Smith, *Frank Lloyd Wright* (1992), 18-19.

16. Geddes, *Miracle in the Evening*, 153.

17. Hugh Morrison, *Louis Sullivan: Prophet of Modern Architecture* (New York: W.W. Norton, 1963), 80-110; and Meryl Secrest, *Frank Lloyd Wright* (New York: Knopf, 1993), 107.

18. Edward Gordon Craig, "To Eleonora Duse" (1908), reprinted in Craig, *The Theatre – Advancing* (Boston: Little, Brown, 1928), 243.

19. See George Bernard Shaw, "Mainly About Myself," preface to *Plays Pleasant and Unpleasant* (1898); and Shaw, *The Intelligent Woman's Guide to Socialism and Capitalism* (1928).

20. Starr, *Inventing the Dream*, 64-98; 199-234.

21. Aline Barnsdall, quoted in Geddes, *Miracle in the Evening*, 156.

22. Frank Lloyd Wright, *An Autobiography* (New York: Horizon Press, 1977), 250-51.

The Architect

1. Wright, *Autobiography*, 67-68.
2. Ibid., 191-95.
3. Wright, "Some Aspects of the Past and Present of Architecture," in Baker Brownell and Frank Lloyd Wright, *Architecture and Modern Life* (New York: Harper & Bros., 1937), 17.
4. Wright, quoted by John H. Howe, in *Frank Lloyd Wright Remembered* (Washington, D.C.: Preservation Press, 1991), 118.
5. Wright, "Some Aspects of the Past…," 17.
6. Ibid., 21.
7. See "The Client," Note 1.
8. Barnsdall to Wright (July 27, 1916), in Smith, *Frank Lloyd Wright* (1992), 22.
9. See Smith, *Frank Lloyd Wright* (1992), 41, Figure 4-4; and Neil Levine, "Hollyhock House and the Romance of Southern California," *Art in America* (September, 1983), 163.
10. Wright, *Autobiography*, 251.
11. Smith, *Frank Lloyd Wright* (1992), 50.
12. Secrest, *Frank Lloyd Wright*, 209.
13. Wright, *Autobiography*, 189.
14. See Esther McCoy, *Vienna to Los Angeles: Two Journeys*.
15. David Gebhard and Harriette Von Breton, *Lloyd Wright, Architect.* Exhibition catalog, Art Galleries, University of California, Santa Barbara, November 23–December 22, 1971. Lloyd Wright had studied engineering and agronomy at the University of Wisconsin at Madison before interrupting his studies to join his father in Italy, in 1909-1910.
16. In the early 1930s, Barnsdall's daughter, Aline Elizabeth, studied under Wright as a Taliesin fellow. See Smith, *Frank Lloyd Wright* (1992), 195.
17. Lloyd Wright, conversation with Neil Levine, in Levine, "Hollyhock House," 160.
18. Barnsdall to Norman Bell Geddes (July 4, 1916), in Smith, *Frank Lloyd Wright* (1992), 23.
19. Barnsdall, quoted in Florence Lawrence, "Eminence to Be Made Rare Beauty Spot," *Los Angeles Examiner*, July 6, 1919, in Smith, *Frank Lloyd Wright* (1992), 50.
20. Wright, "Some Aspects of the Past…," 18.

Photography Credits

The use of historic photographs and drawings was made possible through the courtesy of:

Page 4
The City of Los Angeles, Departments of Recreation and Parks and Cultural Affairs.

Page 6
© 1996
The Frank Lloyd Wright Foundation

Page 9
California Historical Society, Title Insurance and Trust Photo Collection, Department of Special Collections, University of Southern California Library

Page 11
Michael Devine

Page 14
Security Pacific National Bank Photograph Collection/Los Angeles Public Library

Page 18
© 1996
The Frank Lloyd Wright Archives

Page 21
© 1996
The Frank Lloyd Wright Foundation

Page 23
© 1996
The Frank Lloyd Wright Foundation

Page 25
The City of Los Angeles, Departments of Recreation and Parks and Cultural Affairs

Page 27
© 1996
The Frank Lloyd Wright Foundation

Page 29
Bruce Torrence Historical Collection

Page 31
© 1996
The Frank Lloyd Wright Foundation

Page 33
Levin and Associates

Page 41
The City of Los Angeles, Departments of Recreation and Parks and Cultural Affairs

Master Plan Drawings
William Johnson